Life-Changing
Messages

Life-Changing Messages

Remarkable Stories from the Other Side

GORDON SMITH

HAY HOUSE

Australia • Canada • Hong Kong • India
South Africa • United Kingdom • United States

Essex County Council Libraries

Fi.... .... by:
Hay House UK Ltd, 292B Kensal Rd, London W10 5BE.
Tel.: (44) 20 8962 1230; Fax: (44) 20 8962 1239. www.hayhouse.co.uk

Published and distributed in the United States of America by:
Hay House, Inc., PO Box 5100, Carlsbad, CA 92018-5100.
Tel.: (1) 760 431 7695 or (800) 654 5126; Fax: (1) 760 431 6948 or (800) 650 5115.
www.hayhouse.com

Published and distributed in Australia by:
Hay House Australia Ltd, 18/36 Ralph St, Alexandria NSW 2015.
Tel.: (61) 2 9669 4299; Fax: (61) 2 9669 4144. www.hayhouse.com.au

Published and distributed in the Republic of South Africa by:
Hay House SA (Pty), Ltd, PO Box 990, Witkoppen 2068.
Tel./Fax: (27) 11 467 8904. www.hayhouse.co.za

Published and distributed in India by:
Hay House Publishers India, Muskaan Complex, Plot No.3, B-2,
Vasant Kunj, New Delhi – 110 070.
Tel.: (91) 11 41761620; Fax: (91) 11 41761630. www.hayhouse.co.in

Distributed in Canada by:
Raincoast, 9050 Shaughnessy St, Vancouver, BC V6P 6E5.
Tel.: (1) 604 323 7100; Fax: (1) 604 323 2600

© Gordon Smith, 2007

Design by Leanne Siu

Typeset by e-Digital Design

The moral rights of the author have been asserted.

The author of this book does not dispense medical advice or prescribe the use of
any technique as a form of treatment for physical or medical problems without
the advice of a physician, either directly or indirectly. The intent of the author is
only to offer information of a general nature to help you in your quest for
emotional and spiritual wellbeing. In the event you use any of the information
in this book for yourself, which is your constitutional right, the author and the
publisher assume no responsibility for your actions.

A catalogue record for this book is available from the British Library.

ISBN 978-1-4019-1567-4

Printed and bound in Great Britain by TJ International, Padstow, Cornwall.

Dedication

I would like to dedicate this book to my friend
Julie Thacker Scully – for all her efforts in trying
to bring knowledge of the continuation of the
human spirit to the minds of many the world over.

Acknowledgements

I would like to thank Lizzie Hutchins for all her hard work, and Chris Hutchins for accompanying me on many of my journeys.

Also my friend Keith Bishop – who reminds me to stay forever young; and Derek Lambias, one of the kindest men I have ever met.

And last but by no means least, Louise L. Hay, a true lady of spirit.

Contents

Chapter 1: The right words at the right time   1

Chapter 2: When even hope starts to fade...   19

Chapter 3: Confirmation from spirit   39

Chapter 4: Crossing language barriers   51

Chapter 5: Seeing is believing   63

Chapter 6: Take the love...   75

Chapter 7: Talking to the 'well-connected'   93

Chapter 8: Living life with spirit   109

Chapter 9: Finding those in need   135

Chapter 10: Trusting in spirit   153

Chapter 11: Dreams, nightmares and fears   163

Chapter 12: Words of proof   175

Chapter 13: The message that changed my own life   187

CHAPTER 1

The right words at the right time

ANYONE who has ever received a message from the spirit world is likely to tell you that it changed their life. Can anything be more comforting than to hear from someone for whom you have been grieving, someone you believed had gone forever? To hear that that person is very much alive and happy on the other side, free of pain, guilt and remorse and very much in touch with what is going on in your life is an extraordinary experience, especially when it is backed up by 'evidence' – secrets, perhaps, that only you and that person could possibly have known.

During the course of my mediumship I have had had the privilege of delivering thousands of messages, and the joy of seeing the way they affect the recipients. I am merely the messenger; I pass on what I receive and then move on. But what always stays with me is the way the recipients change.

During a recent trip to Greece I was giving a press conference when a middle-aged lady who had managed to squeeze herself in called out from the back of the room. She was dressed all in black and looked as though she had been mourning all her life. What she was saying, according to my Greek translator, was the equivalent of 'Help me, help me! I am desperate.' Now the point of such a gathering is to explain to the media what I do, not to demonstrate it. But this woman was clearly suffering greatly and I asked her to stay right where she was because once the conference was over, I would certainly do my best to help.

I learned later that she was the mother of a teenager she had reported missing over 20 years ago. When her daughter's body was eventually found the initial police report suggested she had died from a drugs overdose – just another addict to clutter up their books. However, her mother could not accept that that was the case. As the press filed out (leaving one television cameraman she had allowed to film the sitting), this much-troubled lady took a seat in front of me.

Almost immediately her daughter came through. She told me she knew her mother believed she had been raped and murdered and that she was correct. Furthermore, she gave information about the people responsible. Tears ran down the lady's cheeks, but she simply nodded as I passed on her daughter's message.

Her daughter knew what lengths her mother had gone to over the years in a bid to uncover the truth. She had infiltrated the team of undesirables she always believed had been responsible, even acting the part of a prostitute at one point in order to find out more about the gang. Justice had never been done, but it would be. The daughter was pointing to her nails. At first I didn't understand what this meant, but her mother smiled. Then the girl told me that her body had been exhumed and traces of hair and flesh had been found underneath her fingernails, leading police to investigate one of the suspects her mother had pointed to.

With a trial pending I obviously cannot pass on here the names that she gave me. That isn't important. What does matter is that she told her mother she was not suffering; indeed, she was happy and smiling down on her. Her mother went away happy for the first time in over 20 years. I am told that today she no longer wears black and is enjoying resuming a normal way of life.

Who could deny that this was a message that changed a life?

*****

I rarely get the opportunity to see the long-term results of my work, but on the occasions that I do, I am never disappointed. Readers of my last book, *Stories From The Other Side*, will recall I mentioned an Indian lady who called out from the audience at a demonstration I was giving at a large hall in the Midlands. She cried out, 'But that's my son, my son!' when I started to give a message to the wrong person. That can happen in a crowded hall. On this occasion I had been offering the message to a woman who was sitting in front of her.

Initially the Indian lady was crying uncontrollably, but when she recovered her composure she said, 'A few minutes ago I asked my son for a sign. "If you're here," I said, "knock something over," and at that very moment the lady sitting next to me spilled her drink.'

The message that came through was a lovely one. The boy told me it was almost a year since he had passed and that his school was preparing a memorial to him, a stone to be consecrated in his memory. There was more, much more, and each time I relayed the boy's words his mother screamed, 'Yes, yes, yes!'

Finally I heard myself saying, 'Your son says, "Don't let my death ruin your life and please put away those thoughts of killing yourself."'

When the demonstration ended, the woman and her husband approached me at the back of the hall. She was laughing and sobbing at the same time and then she turned to her husband and said, 'My husband doesn't even know this, but if my son hadn't come through tonight I was going to kill myself tomorrow. Everything you told me was accurate and I know that his spirit is living. Thank you, thank you, thank you.'

Then her husband said, 'Gordon Smith has saved my wife's life tonight. She came here so miserable and she is going away so happy. She knows now without any doubt that there is life on the other side and our son is living it.'

I must admit that I worried for some time about this lady. There was no doubt that her son had given me a detailed and loving message for her, but when a person is as suicidal as she was that night there is the danger that they could return to their old suicidal ways as time passes. So I was pleased when the couple asked to see me again a year later. I rarely give a second reading, but I was so relieved that this lady was very much alive.

Almost immediately I came up with an Indian name which I had certainly never heard before.

'I nearly fell off my chair,' the woman said later. 'How could you have known about that person? We are Sikhs and that isn't even a Sikh name, yet you pronounced it perfectly. I could have fainted!'

She told me that the name was that of a girl who had been a friend of her son's in the sixth form at school. One day he had found her looking disconsolate in the playground and had tried to comfort her. 'What's the matter?' he had asked her gently. The girl had explained that her cousin had recently passed over and she was missing him dreadfully. 'Why don't you talk to him?' the woman's son suggested. 'It'll make you feel better.'

'Weren't you listening!' his friend demanded. 'He's passed away. He's dead!'

'I know that,' said the boy. 'But he can still hear you. Try talking to him, you'll see.'

The woman told me that she has seen the girl since her son died and that she now talks to her cousin every day and feels so much better.

And there was more to rock this lady on her chair.

I told her that I sensed something strange to do with her son and a telephone.

'How could you know about that?!' she exclaimed.

It turned out that she had been watching UK Living one night shortly after her son had passed over and had seen the US medium John Edward. He had been talking to a bereaved mother whose son had attempted to contact her by making her telephone ring inexplicably. The Indian lady had thought no more about it and when, half an hour later, her phone had rung, she had answered it normally. There had been silence at the other end of the line. After a few moments she had hung up and then dialled 1471.

'Normally if you've been called ex-directory or from abroad there's a recorded announcement telling you what's occurred,' she pointed out. 'But this time there was nothing. Dead silence. It was so strange.'

I was able to inform her that it had probably been her son trying to give her a sign.

But there was more. Next I told her that I was picking up a woman, someone not particularly close to her family, who had died very recently. 'Your son helped her to pass over,' I told her.

'That's amazing too!' she said. 'She was a friend of my mother-in-law's. I didn't know her very well, but I visited her in hospital. She died just a few days ago and last night I said a prayer to my son and asked him to help her pass over!'

That was great evidence, but I seemed to draw a blank with the next thing I saw: a cute little puppy with long spaniel ears. No matter how hard they tried, the couple couldn't recall such a dog in their or their son's life – he had actually been afraid of dogs. I told them not to worry and not to try to make a connection. Maybe it would all become clear later. And that's just what happened. A day or two afterwards the lady was chatting on the phone to her husband's sister, who lived in Holland. 'Oh,' she said. 'I was coming out of the hairdresser's and my husband said he'd seen just the dog for me – a little spaniel with long ears!'

Back in the sitting with the couple, I got such a strong sense of this boy's purity and goodness that I felt moved almost to tears.

'I feel your son was almost too good for this world,' I told his parents. 'He tells me that he feels such pity for everyone.'

'He always tried to help people when he was alive,' they told me.

'Well, that's what he's doing now,' I revealed. 'I see

him surrounded by hundreds of children. He's helping them to pass over. That's what he spends his time doing!'

This couple will never forget their wonderful son and I will never forget them – a mother on the verge of suicide and a father at the end of his tether whose lives were so dramatically changed by the message I was privileged to give them that night in Leamington Spa.

*****

One young man who made a point of contacting me later to tell me just how much the messages I had given him during a demonstration in Margate, Kent, had changed his life was one Michael Lenihan. I had never met him before, and had it not been for the fact that he recorded the message, I could never have remembered it. So I am indebted to him for the accuracy of the report that follows.

That night a mother came through who had passed away in hospital about two years earlier. I could clearly see her surrounded by what looked like relatives. 'All except one,' she told me. She kept repeating the number 7. She mentioned a baby that had been born since she passed over and she heard everyone saying they wished she had been there to see it. She wanted to say that she had seen it and was delighted with it. I saw something too – a gold cross that she was holding in her hand.

Now let's let Michael pick up the story:

The gathering at the bedside did of course take place and there was indeed one missing. My brother, who lives in Canada, came home when my mother was very ill but had to return before she died, and missed the funeral – something he deeply regrets. The amazing thing here is that on the very night she died he was attending Gordon's demonstration in Vancouver – an event he had booked tickets for prior to Mammy getting sick.

As for the number 7 Mammy kept repeating, I have seven brothers and sisters and was the seventh child born to her. There were seven of us around that bed when she passed. The new baby, Joshua, was christened in Dublin on 21 April 2007 and I know Mammy was there with us. And the gold cross, it was Mammy's and I carry it everywhere tucked safely away in my wallet. I showed it to Gordon afterwards, but of course he was not surprised.

I told Michael his mammy was very proud of him and was pleased he kept the picture of her smiling. He said:

I know the picture Mammy referred to. It was taken at the surprise seventieth birthday my younger brother David and I threw for her. Mammy is smiling in it and David keeps a copy of it in a prominent place and I do too. And every night before we go to bed in our separate houses – he lives in Dublin – we talk to her and kiss the pictures.

Michael's mammy also told me about an office where she had looked over his shoulder while he was working. She mentioned Galway Bay, music, a piano, the names Ray and Simon, a birthday two days previously and the signing of a document.

Michael:

I worked from home for seven years, turning my boxroom into an office, and Mammy would come and watch me at work. Galway Bay brings back memories of a very happy trip. I took my elder sister Alice and her husband Pat and Mammy, of course, to see the world Irish Championships and it was when we got home that I told Mammy I was gay. It was a vulnerable time in my life, but Mammy just hugged me and told me I was her son and she loved me unconditionally. Music? I thought about David, who is a musician, but he mainly plays the guitar. Then I remembered that I had promised to take piano lessons this year. Ray is a close friend of mine. Simon is my next-door neighbour (his mum was sitting next to me at the demonstration) and his birthday was two days earlier. I didn't know it, but in the interval Simon turned to me and said he was leasing a new car and had signed the contract that very day. How accurate is all that?

Michael's mum was a talkative lady. She went on to mention New York, horses, a younger person named Brian and a Kath, and she wanted to know why Michael wasn't wearing his glasses.

Michael:

Sitting on my left was my best friend Jane and on my right my partner Peter. The three of us went to New York together in 1989 and Mammy enjoyed watching our videos and pictures of that trip. My first-ever job was at an Irish stud farm looking after yearlings. As Mammy knows, horses are my favourite animals. I couldn't think of a Brian, but my eldest sister knew very well whom Gordon was talking about. Kath was a family friend from Ireland and she had us over the previous Thursday for a traditional Irish dinner and we had talked about Mammy, so no doubt she was there with us. I use glasses now, but only for VDU work, so that's why I didn't have them on at the hall.

Michael's mammy then talked about a dark period he had gone through following her passing. She had helped him through it and wanted him to know she would always be with him.

Michael:

I understood. My mum had been my best friend and there had been a couple of occasions when I wished to join her on the other side. But I know she is around me and with the help of my partner Peter and my very close friends, I have managed to learn to live with her passing.

Twenty-four of my friends from Wickham Lane Spiritualist church in south-east London were in the congregation with me that night and can vouch for the information Gordon gave me. The great significance of the message for me was that it has restored my faith in mediumship and I now feel I can return to platform work myself to help others just as Gordon helped me.

Michael's mother had been his best friend, but imagine the effect of getting a message from the closest of relatives you never really knew. That happened to Moira Collins, who also lived in London. She had been just 14 months old when her father Jack had died, so he was virtually a complete stranger to her. But when she came to see me and I contacted the spirit world to see who, if anyone, had a message for her, it was Jack who came through.

I, of course, had no idea who it was she wanted to hear from, but I knew that the bereavement that troubled her had not been a recent one.

'This man has been on the other side for a long time,' I told her. Then he gave me some more details. 'It's your dad,' I went on. 'He died young and you never really knew him.'

'That's right,' Moira said. 'My father, Jack, passed away when I was 14 months old. Sadly I've no memory of him, but I always say a few words to him every now and then and when something goes right I'm convinced he has had a hand in it.'

'Jack says, "Yes, I do know what's happening. I do see things,"' I told Moira. 'And he knows about your plans for this year. Spiritually, he'll be with you. Now I'm picking up images of photographs that you have looked at recently and see he was a very handsome man. He's with your grandmother. She died after him. She has a sense of excitement and says, "I will be there." A wedding is coming up. "It's going to be fabulous," she says. "I'll make my presence known."'

'That's my nana, Kathleen. I'm so pleased she's come through as well,' said Moira.

'I can see two other young women standing beside you,' I told her. 'Your dad's showing me the three of you dressed for a wedding. You also have a brother – your dad's proud of what he's achieved. You've all come to a point in your lives where something big is happening. Someone is moving or expanding their house. This year life will blossom for the whole family.'

'He's seeing my two sisters, Gillian and Claire,' Moira said, 'and they're dressed for a wedding because they were both married recently. My brother Simon's just been promoted, which he's proud of, and he's having a baby boy in January – a surprise after two girls. It's my sister who's extending her house.'

'Your father wants to mention your mother,' I continued. 'Her life has changed immensely since he died and he reckons she's done a fabulous job. He wants you to ask her if she's had her tests done. There's an anniversary at the end of December. He's handing over flowers.'

'Yes, she's been for a check-up. She's recovering from Ramsey Hunt Syndrome – it's an ear problem. It's good to know Dad's watching over her. Their wedding anniversary would have been 29 December.'

'There are lots of envelopes to be written. You're a person who tries to manage your life – you plan things.

There have been some uncertainties, but there's a lot of joy in your life to be had this year. Everything will be sorted out by July. Jack knows the date of your wedding was linked to another date – it was picked specifically.'

'He's right. We picked the date so we could be on honeymoon on our birthdays, which are two weeks apart. I never knew how much work went into a wedding – there are certainly a lot of envelopes to write!'

'And there are family connections in Dublin. I can hear people singing.'

'It was my nan who came from Dublin,' said Moira, fondly. 'And yes, she did love a party. I'll look for a sign from her at my wedding.'

'I get a lovely feeling,' I was glad to be able to tell her. 'You are at a good point in your life. A very positive message is being brought forward.'

'It's so comforting,' she said, 'to know that loved ones are still aware of our lives and very proud of us.'

*****

Moira went away happy, as do so many of the weeping, grieving, often suicidal people I address at meetings, but they are not the only ones to do so. Passing on messages from spirit is an amazing experience for me too. It's a real buzz and I am lifted by it. It's like unlocking a secret, something that's been held in really tight – like opening a box and saying, 'Wow, look what's in there!'

I have to try and do it as quickly as I can and then ground myself, because if I were to try and retain what I have seen and heard from the other side I wouldn't be able to go out and do it all over again the next day. My head would be too full and I am, after all, only the spirit messenger. 'Deliver it, but don't dwell on it,' has to be my modus operandi.

Although what I do is very different from, say, what a rock star does up on stage in front of a large crowd, I wouldn't be human if I failed to be elated by the demonstration of my gift. And, as I have said before, I am no saint, and when I leave a theatre or a hall after a particularly successful evening, I like to go out and have a drink or go to a party. That might seem strange to people who find it hard to understand the connection between happiness and talking to the dead, but the messages do bring such happiness, and the energy that flows through me can be incredible – as is the thought of bringing help to those who are grieving.

CHAPTER 2

When even hope starts to fade...

WHEN someone asks me if I can help find a loved one who is missing, I always warn them that if I do make contact it will mean that the loved one is dead, and I ask, 'Are you ready for that?'

This happened in the case of Mrs Sally Perrin when she came to see me for a private sitting some time ago. She said she understood and, yes, she was prepared for such a sad eventuality.

A young man came through almost immediately. I remember describing him – he had light-coloured hair and normally wore glasses, although he did not have them on when he passed over. She said that was just how he looked. I said he was telling me there was a connection to the army, that he knew his mother had been looking for him and that his remains would be found in a river, on the bend of the river, in fact, and because I could hear a torrent of water, I believed it was close to a weir. She asked me to ask him about the circumstances of his death, and what I got back from the other side was that although it wasn't murder there had been a cover-up by people on this side who knew the details but weren't going to tell anyone anything.

Let Sally take up the story:

My son Blake went missing on 8 August 2004. He had just finished his second term at Sandhurst Military Training College and he was leading eight other lads on an army adventure-training expedition. He was a very experienced mountaineer and was a qualified leader, having passed the appropriate courses. They set off in three cars for France on the Friday, which was his twenty-fifth birthday, and stopped that night in St Omer before driving down the following day to Chamonix. They pitched their tents and some of them then went for a run up along the river path. They then had a couple of beers before going into town for a meal. Walking into Chamonix they crossed a tributary to the river L'Arve and as Blake had been whitewater-rafting there during a three-month stay the previous year, he warned them about how dangerous the river was in the summer when the torrent was in full spate from the melting mountain snows and glaciers. He pointed out that if any of them went in they'd be unlikely to survive because of the extremely cold temperature of the water; it is consistently 3–5 degrees, summer and winter. He was a very responsible young man and very knowledgeable about the area.

After dinner they went to several bars and finished up at a nightclub, which he and another guy left at around 2.30–3 a.m. They were pretty happy, but they weren't that drunk, I've been assured. They walked back to the campsite, which is well-lit and well-signed, but it is alleged that Blake decided it wasn't the campsite, so he marched off down the road and the other guy followed him until he disappeared into a garden, whereupon the other guy said, 'Oh, I'm not following him in there.' (They were very close to the river at this point, only ten yards away.) The other guy went marching down the road, expecting Blake to come out the other side, but he never appeared and that's the last he saw of him. The guy went back to the campsite eventually and told the others and they said, 'Not to worry, he'll turn up in the morning,' so the police were not informed until mid-afternoon on the Sunday and nobody called me until 8 o'clock that night.

My first reaction was to fly directly out there, which my husband David (Blake's stepfather) and I did, despite the army saying there was no need for us to go. We spent the whole of that week searching with his cousins and some of his closest friends, sometimes pulling at the river debris with our bare hands. The police said they couldn't use search dogs because there had been a heavy storm the night before and that there would be no scent. In any case their view seemed to be that he was drunk and had fallen in the river and that was the end of it as far as they were concerned. He may have been a bit merry, but his method of dealing with that would have been to lie down and sleep it off. He was so aware of how dangerous that river could be. You don't just see it; you smell it and you can certainly hear it. It's a fearsome, horrible river – I know because my husband and I had been staying nearby three weeks earlier and I'd called David's attention to it, saying it gave me the creeps.

As well as physically searching, we got hundreds of missing-person posters printed up and we distributed them initially throughout the whole valley of Chamonix so everybody locally was aware of Blake's disappearance. We also made appeals on TV and via the radio stations. Then the police started saying, 'This is really unusual. You usually find some trace of a person who's gone in the river,' so we thought, 'Well, maybe he's still alive and has just wandered off somewhere,' and we got in touch with the Missing Persons helpline and then we got posters distributed throughout France, Switzerland, Spain and Italy, and because Chamonix is close to the borders we had postcards printed in three languages and got long-distance lorry drivers to distribute them throughout Europe. We emailed everybody we and our friends could think of, contacting thousands of people, and set up a website.

We have been out there seven times now and have done everything we can think of, including locating a machine (called a side-scan sonar) that looks into water and through sand at great depths (that proved impractical because the water was too fast-moving) and finding tracker dogs in the Hague that are specially trained to find bodies in deep water. Then suddenly the French police announced they had such dogs and provided us with two of the nation's three handlers and five of the seven dogs for two whole days, during which we searched from dawn till dusk.

Alas, it was all to no avail and that's when I decided to turn to the psychic side of things. I was not a Spiritualist, but I've always had an open mind and thought there must be something in it. That's when somebody recommended Gordon Smith to me: 'He's pretty good,' they said. I found out about a demonstration he was doing in Bristol and a friend and I travelled from my home in Shropshire to see him. In the second half, when he did a question-and-answer session, I thought, 'Now's my chance,' and put up my hand. When Gordon picked me I said, 'Can you help me find my son?' He said,

'Well, this is probably not the right time or place, but talk to me afterwards.' I couldn't reach him afterwards, but a lady from Hay House took my phone number and said he would call me. I didn't think it would happen, but, lo and behold, both she and he subsequently phoned me. He said he would see me at the London hotel where he was then staying, so my friend and I travelled down to see him and he was just amazing. He knew nothing of my story and was very clear that he didn't want to know anything in advance of the sitting, yet when Blake came through he came up with all kinds of information he couldn't possibly have known, and which was spot-on. Interestingly enough, he said the body would be found towards the third anniversary of his death, which is exactly what has happened.

He said the sixth was an important day. Well, obviously that was important because Blake had set off on his ill-fated trip on the sixth and it was his birthday. Gordon had him wearing something yellow like a big Puffa jacket, which was what he always wore when he was mountaineering. Gordon said the thirteenth was a bad news day – and that was the day the search was called off. He also said all this was close to Blake's birthday.

He said he'd got people chatting around Blake in a bar or a nightclub and a new mate he barely knew was with him. He described a raging river with steep banks on either side surrounded by marshy flat land with mountains in the background. Then he said somebody who was close to Blake knew the ___ in of what had happened but wasn't prepared to tell. In fact, there had been a bizarre cover-up. This is what we've always thought.

Thanks to publicity surrounding yet another visit to France, a man called Joseph Dancet contacted us last May to say he had seen Blake's body in the river ten days after he had disappeared and had informed the police about it, although they hadn't told us for another five months. Because of this he thought the police had not believed him. We assured him that we believed him and he then pledged that he and his friend Claude Antoine would do everything they could to help us find Blake's remains. So for the next eight months, whenever they had the chance, they would take themselves off to the river with strange-looking rakes and go through the huge amount of debris that had been deposited on the banks during that exceptionally high spate the summer Blake disappeared. They were convinced that his body would be somewhere in that area and with the assistance of some aerial photographs that I managed to track down, we could see where the river had spilled out of its banks that year.

The day before New Year's Eve 2006 we had that break-through. Joseph had found a bone, a human femur, and it was found in exactly the kind of area Gordon had described. Annoyingly, it was found just a few yards further south of the place where every search that we had conducted had ended, just downstream of a bridge that denotes the beginning of the torrent, where, according to the police, bodies do not get caught up! The DNA matched Blake's, so we had confirmed what Gordon had told us – that Blake was dead and his remains were in the river about 60 kilometres south of Chamonix. While we were watching the police divers reconnoitring the area where the bone was discovered, they found two other bones, which are now being examined to try and determine the cause of Blake's death.

I got a great deal of comfort from my sitting with Gordon. He, or rather Blake, gave us a lot of accurate information. He had said his body would be found close to where we had already been searching but in an area in which no particular interest had been shown at the time – in moving water, near a torrent and a weir where the banks were high, etc., etc. It was absolutely bang-on.

But there was more to assure us that Gordon was directly in touch with my son. He said Blake was showing him a photograph of himself abseiling down an ice cliff and telling him I had the photograph close to my phone. I had received just such a photograph from one of his friends, put it in a frame and placed it close to the phone the day before I had gone to see Gordon.

He also said there was some kind of official report about to come out 'and you won't learn a thing from it'. That was the army report, which certainly lived up to Blake's opinion of it. Gordon said he saw a gun dog sitting next to Blake, a very happy dog. The description perfectly matched Star, our dog who had passed over a few years earlier. Blake would often take her for a run. He said there was a tree being planted for him, which was what his father had done in his garden. He referred to cross-country skiing – 'specifically not downhill skiing' – which Blake excelled at and said the number eight loomed large. Well, that was the day he passed over.

Going back to the incident itself, Blake said he was walking along in pitch darkness, amongst trees, with grass underfoot, and someone was walking alongside him. He was not wearing his glasses. Suddenly things got out of hand; there was a huge amount of panic. He was able to pick out a mesh fence – well, the garden he was said to have disappeared from was surrounded by a mesh fence, but that was made up to divert us! 'His glasses are in range of the fence,' Gordon said, but despite raking through the grass and surrounding area until my hands bled, we have never found them. Maybe they are still there somewhere. According to Gordon, Blake was gone before he was put into the water and he was unaware of how this happened. The whole thing is vague, but something happened and it wasn't planned.

Gordon said it was 'orchestrated. Everybody's scared of the conspiracy and they had help to plan [it], but there is a sort of code of honour between the conspirators'. He also told me that a higher-ranking officer knows what happened.

Then he changed the subject and said Blake wanted us to know that he'd be with us on Friday, and that Friday we were travelling through the Welsh mountains that Blake loved to a place called Abersoch on the Welsh coast.

He said, 'Say hello to David,' which is my husband's name (he got on well with David) and that he'd met his great grandfather, whom Gordon described as a military man wearing medals. Well, my grandfather was a much-decorated army major. Gordon knew nothing of all this when we met with him.

He said Blake was happy and wanted us to feel what he was feeling, not what we were. And he said that the lights going on and off and other 'electrical things' were his doing. Well, we've had some really weird goings-on of that sort, especially with alarms. It happened once as I put the phone down after speaking to Gordon subsequent to our meeting. It was really spooky. Once the alarm went so completely mad we had to take the fuse out, and that was just after we had brought some of Blake's clothes back from his dad's house. It always seems to happen at what I would call a coincidental time. It happened just after my grandchild was born and then, when we went to my stepdaughter's home to see the baby, she said, 'Sal, my alarm keeps going off for no reason, it's really

weird.' I said, 'Oh, that's Blake mucking about.' And it is
Blake, according to Gordon, and we like that. Blake always
had a good sense of humour.

I was never the kind of person to believe in these kinds of
happenings and my husband was a huge sceptic, but now he's
a total convert. It's just extraordinary. There was just so much
evidence there from Gordon to prove that it was Blake coming
through to us. Just one example is that he said that at night and
in the morning Blake hears me talking to him, and I do. I say,
'Goodnight, Blake,' and 'Good morning' when I pass his portrait.

Finally, I asked Gordon to say, 'Come on, Blake, we need
to know who's responsible here. How did you end up in the
river? Come on, you've got to tell me.'

His reply was that he did not want to say, there was a
code of honour and it would implicate other people, and that
mistakes happen.

Then Gordon said Blake had drawn a huge letter, which we
believe is the initial of a culprit's name, but I will not disclose
this while the enquiries are still ongoing.

Needless to say, I was delighted to help Sally. Her son
was very clear that he wanted to bring closure to her by
indicating where his earthly remains were to be found –
and that is not always the case, as we shall see in the

next story. He was very strong on information, even down to showing me airline tickets – tickets that his mother would use to fly to America. Sally was in fact heading off there to visit her eldest daughter soon afterwards. But the most important part of his message was that he was happy and he wanted his loved ones to know that so that they could be happy too.

I can't repeat often enough that in dealing with grieving people every day of my life, it is wonderful to see them go away with a smile on their face when a loved one comes through with such a joyous message as the one Sally received.

*****

Not long after my meeting with Sally, a man called out from the Notting Hill Spiritualist church congregation: 'One of my family is missing, can you help?' Afterwards he came up to me and handed me a piece of paper on which he had written his name – Jonathan Lane – and telephone number. Alas, careless human being that I am, I lost it, but if nothing else Jonathan is a persistent man and several months later he tracked me down through my publishers.

When he had called out in the church, bells had started ringing in my head. It was all very reminiscent of Sally asking me if I could find her son. As it turned out, the relative Jonathan was anxious to locate had also gone missing in France and for a moment I wondered if it was the same individual. Alas, this turned out to be a very different story...

As soon as he entered the room it was obvious to me that this wasn't Jonathan's scene. He was a financier, at home with power brokers in the high-rise chrome and dark-wood offices of the City and Canary Wharf, a private pilot as comfortable behind the controls of a light air-craft as a sports car. Yet here he was in a small back room on the top floor of a Notting Hill Gate church with three women and a medium.

It wasn't that Jonathan was narrow-minded – he'd been brought up in Africa, had seen the world and knew that there were strange things in it. He just had absolutely no belief in the spirit realm whatsoever. He was only here because he and his wife, Louise, one of the three women in the room, had been trying everything for two years to help Fiona, another of the women, to find her missing son, Jonathan's cousin Christopher.

But things just weren't working out in the search for Chris – or his body, because that's what they all accepted they were likely to find now. The French police had not been interested in tracking down an Englishman living on his own in a room in a bed-and-breakfast in Annecy. A private detective had drawn a blank. Chris had just vanished from the face of the Earth.

And so here they were in Notting Hill with a psychic barber.

I took Fiona's hand.

'I'm being drawn towards France,' I told her. 'Make any sense?'

'Certainly does.'

'And I'm getting this flying sensation. I'm looking down on mountains and lakes like a vulture soaring on a thermal. It's a wonderful feeling of going up and up and looking down on the world!'

As I said that, Jonathan's disbelief in the spirit world vanished forever. 'Chris had always taken to the skies in one way or another,' he told me later.

'He's taking me to Africa,' I went on, 'Zimbabwe, and he's saying he became a horticulturalist or something similar.'

'Spot-on,' said Jonathan.

Jonathan and Chris had been reasonably close, as cousins go. Jonathan's family were in Kenya, Christopher's in Zimbabwe. Chris had always been passionate about two things: gardening and flying, earth and sky. Fiona, his mother, reckoned he would have been a commercial pilot if it hadn't been for his severe dyslexia. Instead, Chris became a private pilot and an expert in the sport of paragliding – 'jumping off a mountain holding a hand-kerchief over your head,' as Jonathan laughingly described it to me.

'He keeps telling me he's flying like a vulture,' I relayed to them, and they all laughed.

'That's the name of his paragliding club: the Vultures!'

In line with his other passion, Chris set up as a rose-growing consultant, but when the troubles hit Zimbabwe he lost his business and spent a year travelling the world looking for a place to start a paragliding school. He ended up in the French Savoie town of Annecy. Lake Annecy is crystal-clear – reputedly the cleanest lake in Europe – and the beautiful town nestles in the foothills of the French Alps, which are perfect for paragliding. Here Chris took a room in a bed-and-breakfast. It was to be his last home.

Jonathan's wife, Louise, remembered an easygoing man thoroughly at home with the natural world and all it contained. At a Millennium safari get-together in

Africa, she had been heavily pregnant and had gone to her hut to put her two 'brats' to bed when, to her horror, a snake had fallen from the ceiling and vanished behind the chest of drawers. Her brother was no help, but called for Chris, who coolly retrieved the two-foot snake, carried it out of the hut in his arms and deposited it safe and sound on the far bank of a nearby river. 'He was more concerned for the snake than for me!' Louise recalled.

The last time Jonathan and Louise had seen Chris had been in 2004, when he had come over to stay and they had spent an idyllic day out in the Suffolk woodlands, where he had been in his element – or at least one of them. Then in January 2005 he had gone missing.

The proprietors of the Annecy B&B said there had been a Saturday-night dinner which Chris had attended. The next morning, a crisp clear winter Sunday, they had heard the front door slam about 10 o'clock. Chris had gone out, taking nothing with him – none of his paragliding gear, not even an overcoat. He had never been seen again.

Two years of fruitless search had followed, leading finally to my door.

Louise told me that she felt that Chris's spirit had guided them to me. Certainly some strange things had happened since he had vanished.

'He's telling me that you fly planes, you're a pilot,' I said to Jonathan.

'That's right.'

'But you almost crashed and you actually felt Chris saved your life.'

The family looked at one another, aghast.

'This has just happened,' said Jonathan. 'I was flying in a light aircraft and the worst of all things took place: I looked out of the cockpit and another plane was heading straight for me. I thought, "My God, this is it! We're going to crash!" Then suddenly my controls just turned and took me off the collision course and we all thought immediately, "Chris has saved our lives."'

Another inexplicable event had happened when Jonathan and Fiona had been to France to plant a tree in Chris's memory. Fiona remembered that there was a special place where Chris would have liked a mountain-ash tree planted, a magical place he had showed her once. She would know it when she saw it, but had no idea where to look. They had set off for France with an impossibly tight schedule, no tree and no location. Yet, when they got there, Fiona found the exact place almost immediately and discovered that a tree had stood there until falling just four weeks earlier, leaving a hole all ready for a new tree. And just nearby was a nursery with a mountain ash ready for planting! The locals in the village café said that they would be happy to care for the tree, a simple service was held and the tree planted.

It all seemed to have been planned.

Jonathan had visited the B&B that had been Chris's last home and had felt most uneasy. He had spent the night in his cousin's old room, but hadn't slept a wink.

Back in Notting Hill, when I got through to Chris I saw him standing with a man who proved to be his father. His words to me made me sure that Fiona and the Lanes' hopes of my leading them to his body were doomed to disappointment.

What Chris said was: 'Get on with your life. I'm happy in my life, get on with yours.' He told me that he had been moving about, talking to different relations he had left behind. He concluded with the chilling words, 'The deed is done! Get rid of my stuff! Move on!'

Jonathan accepts now that Chris's body will never be found, but feels that his cousin's spirit wants to spare his mother the true and ghastly facts surrounding his death.

I couldn't allay his suspicions. I can usually tell when I am dealing with suicide – there is a sense of despair – but I felt none of this when Chris came through. But I did get a strange sensation of dizziness and then of rushing water.

For Jonathan there are a number of facts surrounding Chris's last night and day that don't add up. He is determined now not to let the matter rest and to get in touch with his cousin again, perhaps in circumstances where Chris feels he can speak more freely.

So, alas, this is an unhappy story that has yet to be concluded.

CHAPTER 3

Confirmation from spirit

AWARE as I am that some of the people who seek my help are sceptical about the work I do, it is gratifying to see them go away happy and contented after they have been put in touch with a loved one against their wildest expectations. In some cases the sheer wealth of detailed information that I can provide, information that I could not possibly have access to in any conventional way, convinces them of the reality of the spirit world.

A recent example that comes to mind is that of a lady called Marcia Donne. As usual, she and I had never met before, I knew nothing about her or her story and we did not talk about anything before the sitting began. I explained to her – as I do with everybody who comes for a sitting, particularly if it's their first time with a medium – that if I didn't get a link I would let her know.

That sometimes happens. Maybe it's not the right time.

To be honest, I am never sure why. But if it's not working, I'll know. And, as I say, the worst-case scenario is that we'll have a conversation. If I do pick up on anybody, all I will be doing is describing them to establish that we know whom we are talking to, and then after that I will ask them if they have a message.

No sooner had I taken Marcia's hand, however, than I picked up two people who were very close to us. There was a woman that I sensed coming forward very, very strongly. She had died from an illness and I could feel her tiredness. I could even feel my own body getting tired.

'She feels like a mum to me,' I told Marcia. 'It feels as though she just wants to put her arms round you and let you know that she is fine. I sense there is a gentleman from the spirit world here as well. I sense the two of them standing together. He was a younger man – someone who lived some time ago and who died very suddenly. It was a great shock to the woman and the rest of the family at the time.

'Now I feel the two of them are actually standing beside you. The woman is singing "Happy Birthday", so that tells me that we are very close to a birthday just now. She is giving me a flower and is trying to say to you that she's fine. You've been thinking you could have done more for her, but she is trying to say to you, "No regrets." Part of you felt helpless when she was ill, but she's thanking you for what you did and she wants you to realize that it was enough.'

Marcia was thrilled. She told me she had come to see me in the hope of getting in touch with her mother, who had died almost a year earlier. She had had a stroke, gone into a coma and lost mental control. She lived on for a year, but she was never herself again. She was – just as I told Marcia – very tired. And also very confused. Marcia would spend whole days with her. Then, when she got home and spoke to her on the telephone, she would hear, 'Oh darling, where have you been? I haven't seen you in ages.'

As a result Marcia beat herself up. She felt she should have been with her mother constantly, even though she knew she had her own family to look after. So to hear her mother say, 'No regrets – just don't do that,' was unbelievably comforting.

As for the 'Happy Birthday', her birthday was on 11 May – very close to the time of her meeting with me – and her brothers and others always sent her flowers on that date.

As for the younger man, Marcia hoped it was her father. He had been killed in an accident, aged 48.

Now a lot of people were coming through for Marcia. As I closed my eyes I could see a whole throng of them coming out of the shadows. It seemed as though there was a whole family building up around her. I told her that her mother was mentioning a brother. 'Tell her I've met my brother,' she was saying to me.

Marcia told me that her mother had seven sisters and two brothers, but it was significant that she was saying 'my brother' because she only ever referred to one of them, John, that way; all the other siblings she called by their names. She and John had been extremely close. They had had a lot of fun and everybody around them had had a good laugh whenever they had been together.

At this point in the sitting I suddenly started singing an Irish song.

'That's a song they sang together!' cried Marcia excitedly.

'And Jan's with her,' I told her. 'She's so surrounded by people it's unbelievable and she needs you to know this and to tell you that nobody could have done more for her than you did. It's as though she's saying, "No regrets. Don't you put your mind through any of that stuff." She wants you to know that it was a blessing in the end that she went. She doesn't want to blame any-body; it was her time to go.'

Marcia said that Jan was John's wife – her mother's sister-in-law. She explained too that her mother had been deeply frustrated by her illness; she wasn't the same person any more. She no longer cared about her appearance, and the fact that Marcia had to do every-thing for her took away her pride. 'Oh,' she would say, 'I could never have imagined you'd be having to do this for me.' And her memory loss was deeply troubling. It was horrendous, a living hell, despite the fact that she had slightly recovered physically. Marcia would have quite logical conversations with her and then it would all be gone. She hated leaving her mother in the care of others and felt she should have been there all the time. So it was wonderful for her to hear her mother say that she didn't have to put herself through 'all that stuff' any more.

'Your mother was so tired at the end,' I said to her. 'It must have been the drugs, because I feel as though at the end I'm going in and out. She felt like that and she didn't like it.'

Marcia agreed. Her mother had been given drugs in hospital and they had made her incredibly tired. They had also affected her walking: she would veer to one side. She hated that. But now everything was different.

'She's alive and happy,' I was pleased to tell Marcia. 'She's saying, "I am not as I was, I am how I used to be." I believe she feels like doing an Irish jig!'

Marcia smiled when she heard that. She told me that whenever her son Alex went to the house her mother would be jigging around him and they would start singing together. She and her brother John had always been great fun – really good company. They had lifted everybody's spirits.

'So suddenly not to be so physically active was a great shock for her,' said Marcia, 'and to know she now feels free is great.'

I asked Marcia's mother to give me a memory and she showed me a photograph in which she was part of a group. It looked like a wedding group and it was obviously taken before she became very ill. She was smiling in the picture and it was as though she was saying, 'Think of me like that.'

Marcia recognized it at once. 'That would be her grandson's wedding in Ireland, which Alex took her to. That's the last group photograph I have of her and, yes, she is smiling in it.'

I carried on. '"I'm in the garden," she's saying. I'm

seeing you there too. It's a lovely setting. I think there's somewhere you used to go that was absolutely beautiful – lovely grounds or gardens. I'm seeing your mother walking beside you there.'

Marcia confirmed she always took her mother into the park gardens near her home and they would walk there together. Since she had passed she had had a feeling of her presence whenever she had gone to that park.

'She's given me a pair of specs for some reason,' I continued. 'There's also a ring. She has a wedding ring and she keeps playing with it. She's taken it off now. There's a memory that she's trying to get across and I don't know whether somebody's got this ring or what, but there's definitely something to do with that ring that she wants to bring back to you. And there's something about earrings too.'

Marcia agreed that her mother had glasses, but the ring – her wedding ring – rang a special bell. During her mother's illness when she got very thin she was always pulling it off and throwing it in the air just as they were going out of the door and then they would have to look for it. Before her mother had her stroke she would spend hours on her appearance, but the stroke changed her personality and after it she just didn't give a damn.

Despite this, Marcia told me, she was always trying to make her look the way she did before the stroke. She had always worn earrings and so Marcia would always put earrings on her, but she would pull them out, or try to.

This was interesting because at one point during the sitting I found myself pulling at my ears and saying, 'Oh, get them out, get them out.'

Marcia was amazed. 'That's what she did!'

'She's met Michael in the spirit world,' I went on. 'Now I'm going to Ireland here, there's a connection to Ireland and that's where you'll find Michael. I want to go to a very beautiful part of Ireland. Somebody has been up to Galway or somewhere like that, because I can see beautiful views of the sea. Somebody did that – they didn't live there, they went there – and they have photographs of it, pictures of Galway Bay. But I've also got to go across to Dublin, because there's a very strong connection there. I just get a lovely sense of happiness. She's a kind woman, the kind of woman who would not have minded helping other folk. And there is also a nurse. Does that make sense?'

Marcia told me that Michael was her uncle, her mother's other brother. Her mother's sister Mary was also married to a Michael, so that was the connection there. As for Ireland, her mother was from Dublin and her father was born in Galway.

'I just get a lovely sense of happiness,' I said again. 'I feel as though she wants you to be happy too. It's as though she's saying, "You've done so much for other people, why aren't you doing more for yourself at the moment and allowing yourself to have contentment? That's what you need to do."'

Marcia said she had been a care worker all her married life and was now ready to retire.

'There is something to do with one year that we are coming up to, perhaps an anniversary,' I told her. 'It's being marked by a single rose, just a long-stemmed red rose, not a huge bouquet of flowers, just one rose.'

Marcia said that on the anniversary of her mother's death she placed a single red rose by her picture in her memory.

So much came through in Marcia's sitting that she found it difficult to take it all in at the time, but when she got home what she had been told really began to sink in. She realized that her mother truly wanted her to know that she didn't want to see her torturing herself because of her death and how she was in the months leading up to it. She knew Marcia had been so good to her in life and wanted her to move on and allow herself to be happy.

It dawned on Marcia that all of the information that had come through could only have come from her mother. Better than that, it meant that her mother had access to all her memories again – something that had bothered Marcia at the end of her mum's life when she had found it hard to remember her own family.

Also, she was uplifted to know that her mother was truly concerned about her and the guilt she was feeling. She was delighted to realize that she knew so much of what had occurred in the family since her passing. That was what really changed Marcia's thoughts on life after death and lifted her depression. She knew now that she could get on with her own life, safe in the knowledge that her beloved mother was coping on the other side.

Although she had arrived at the sitting somewhat sceptical, Marcia could find no way of denying that the information that came through was very specific and highly detailed – more detailed than she expected. The healing that she experienced was also completely unexpected. She concluded to me in a letter some weeks later that the message from her mother had definitely changed her life.

I see so many people who start out thinking that what they are about to experience through my mediumship won't make a lot of difference to how they feel. My greatest joy is to learn later that they have turned a corner in their grief and begun to live again.

CHAPTER 4

Crossing language barriers

TRAVELLING to new countries to do what I do is always something of a challenge – particularly ones where English is not the first language. My recent visit to Greece was one such instance – a five-day trip that was, I am happy to say, packed with highly successful demonstrations despite the fact that I obviously had to work through a translator.

At a press conference in Thessaloniki, I had an interesting discourse with journalists who filled a fair-sized room at the Electra Palace hotel. Their questions were well-thought-out and did not once border on the cynical. They asked me why I was such a happy person and I told them when you realize there's no such thing as death, there is nothing to be unhappy about. How did I stay so grounded? When you have got out of bed every day for 23 years to go to work as a barber, that grounds you. Why had I quit being a barber? Queues of people outside my shop in Glasgow – which was already full of people who didn't need a haircut – had made me realize that devoting my life to mediumship was the way to go. One lady wanted to know if I used my gift to make money. I was grateful for that question, as it gave me the opportunity to explain that I never charged for sittings. How could you put a price on putting a grieving mother in touch with her child? 'I earn my living,' I said, 'by writing books, and I am paid by my publishers for the theatre demonstrations that I do.'

And so it went on. I told the distinguished body of interrogators that the whole basis for my work was to provide proof that the people coming through to me from the spirit world were who they said they were by relaying information such as names, dates, details of how they died and evidence of what they had left behind.

To the questioner who wanted to know how involved I got in the grieving process of the people who came to me, I said I had learned from experience (and some tough advice from the highly respected medium Albert Best) to step aside. I would not be helping by shedding tears. I also had to learn to live as normal a life as possible outside my work. If I tried to be a medium 24 hours a day, constantly listening to voices from the other side, I'd be locked away.

I gave details of the scientific tests I had undertaken with Professor Archie Roy at Glasgow University among others, tests that had provided me with proof of evidential accuracy when I had given readings to people who had not even been in the same building and had named people and circumstances in the lives of individuals for whom I had been given no more than the number of the seat they were occupying in a distant hall.

Did I need photographs of the deceased, or items that had belonged to them? No, and although some mediums do it I didn't even need physical contact with whomever I was helping, other than perhaps holding their hand to comfort them.

Could I always make contact with the spirits sought by those who came to see me? No again. Spirits will only come through for those they know to be ready. It wouldn't matter if someone went to a medium every day; if they weren't ready to receive a message, then a spirit would not deliver one. During a demonstration I get drawn towards the people who are ready to receive messages. Furthermore, the strength and evidence of any message depend on how good a communicator the person delivering it is. Some people are able to pass on highly detailed information very clearly, while others find it harder to get the message across. I just stand in the middle and relay what is imparted to me.

To a reporter who wanted to know how I was able to communicate with the spirit of someone who had never spoken English, I explained that communication could come in many forms. Sometimes messages were spoken, sometimes I saw images and sometimes the communication came through feelings that I had learned to interpret over the years. All mediums work very much with their sixth sense.

Sometimes, though, a person who speaks another language will convey sounds to me and I will pass these on as words. Once, in Italy, a boy said two or three words that meant nothing to me and I passed them on to his mother. The translator looked extremely shocked and said, 'Do you realize you have just sworn at the woman in the most profane manner?' However, the mother made it clear that these were the last words her son had said to her during a bitter row before he went to be with a woman who subsequently murdered him, a woman his mother had tried to prevent him from seeing.

I just say what comes into my head.

Back in Greece, I explained how unfair it is when people accuse the likes of me of being cultists who call up the devil. We work for God. And we work long and hard to discipline our minds and perfect our skills. We are also helped by those spirits we consider our guardians, our 'spirit guides' as they are commonly called. These are very highly evolved, angelic and very pure beings, and when people like myself connect with them we bring through their pure light to brighten people's lives. It's a beautiful thing.

I told the journalists that what I did was help people heal and, through my charity work, raise money to heal others. It was important to get that message across, as there are so many misconceptions about mediumship – as there are about life after death.

'Our life force,' I told another writer, 'is what goes on after the death of the body. Where it goes next is a far more free and positive place. Here on Earth is the worst place for a spirit to live and it is no easy matter to come back into this dense, heavy atmosphere.'

Someone else wanted to know about reincarnation and, as I always do when questioned on this subject, I referred her to Buddhism. Buddhists are experts in reincarnation. To them it is simply a truth, not a matter for speculation. In the Western world reincarnation is often seen as somewhat frightening because of the belief that it does away with the individual personality. People think that it will be the end of them, that they will be someone else. But ask the Dalai Lama, who has reincarnated 16 times – each time as the Dalai Lama. And Buddhists will tell you that it is a most selfless act to keep coming into this world when you have reached the level of development that he has and could easily evolve in the life hereafter.

I am also often asked if we go, or risk going, to purgatory when we die. No, this is purgatory here on Earth. And thankfully we will all leave it one day.

*****

At one of the demonstrations I gave there was a particularly happy message for an Athens housewife who had lost her husband. She wept as I gave her his love and passed on some kind words to his children, then she became almost hysterical when he showed me a watch of his which she turned out to be wearing. He may have made his widow cry, but he made me laugh with some of the things he said, yet minutes later I had to choke back a tear myself when he told me how proud he was of the way she had handled things since he passed. When he mentioned a 'special tree', she knew he was referring to one she had planted in his memory.

Another lady's sister came through to talk to her about a ring she had lost and told her exactly where to find it. I like passing on practical messages like that – they are useful as well as consoling.

And then there was another weeping widow, Marie, whose husband had died of a stomach illness – I know, because, as often happens, I got terrible stomach ache as I received his message. He let me know that he had lost an awful lot of weight before he died and I could feel the pain.

And so it went on. There was a spirit who said that the man receiving the message had her stick ('Yes, I do. I have her walking stick with me here and now,' was the translator's version of his reply), a woman clutching a baby which had not lived very long but was now safe and happy, and a music-loving youth who made me feel really tired and drained to show that he had suffered a drugs-related death, although he was anxious to point out that he had not meant to kill himself.

Time and time again the messages concluded, as they usually do, with, 'Stop crying, get on with your life and be happy, because I am.' That is the message that so often changes people's lives.

*****

I had been warned to expect opposition from religious circles during my stay in Greece, but what happened at the end of the trip was quite the opposite. As I was travelling to Athens airport to catch my flight back to London, my Greek publisher, Emmanuela Nikolaidou, took a call on her mobile phone. She was clearly surprised when the caller identified himself, but as she handed me the phone, she said only, 'It's for you, Gordon.'

The voice at the other end of the line was that of a cultured man: 'Mr Smith, I have followed with great interest what you have been doing in our country. I support your work very much. I hope you will return as our guest and I would be most grateful if you would agree to see some people I know who have recently suffered a tragic loss. I feel sure you can help them.'

The caller was connected to the Greek Orthodox Church, yet he had taken the trouble to discover my whereabouts and the number on which he eventually reached me. I was heartened by his support.

*****

I returned from Greece ecstatic at the warm reception I had received, but exhausted from the sheer intensity of the tumultuous happenings of the previous five days, particularly on the testing live-television shows I had been required to submit myself to in order to earn my right of passage in the country.

The morning following my return I learned that I was to give three readings to some deeply grieving people.

The first was a woman in her early forties who came in accompanied by her husband. From the intensity of her grief, you might have thought she had lost a husband, or a child, but all I could sense around her was her grandmother. Fortunately, after I had told her that her grandmother was happy in the next world, she said that that was the only person she had lost and wanted to hear from.

'Your gran is telling me you have her engagement ring with you,' I said.

The woman, crying gently, pulled open the top buttons of her dress and pulled out a gold chain, at the end of which was the very ring.

Her husband was clearly delighted and confirmed

everything I had passed on. He told me afterwards that his wife was 'greatly uplifted' by the experience.

Next came one of the most detailed messages I had been party to for quite some time. It was for a couple who were sitting before me, clearly distraught and saying nothing.

I said, 'You've lost a son and he's here with us right now. He tells me his name is Luke.'

Again I was confronted with the all-too-familiar sound of a woman sobbing as she nodded affirmation.

'Oh, God,' I thought, 'a boy has died,' and I prayed silently for the help of my old friend Albert Best, who was always particularly good when children were involved.

'Luke is telling me you had just bought him a bicycle for his fifteenth birthday and that when he took it out on the road, a van hit him and killed him. In addition to the name "Luke" he is calling out the name "Sam" and is showing me twins. Why is he showing me twins?'

The woman gasped. The circumstances of his death were correct, her name was Sam and his father was a twin, she said.

Luke went on to send his best regards to his younger brother and his love to Max, who turned out to be his cat. He left with a daunting message: 'You're not going to get justice on this accident, I'm afraid. Someone is getting away with it.'

At the end of the session the couple told me that the van driver had been told he would not be prosecuted.

The third sitting was for a woman in her fifties whose husband came through and told me he had died very recently of a heart attack. He too supplied some really good evidence. 'He says he's pleased with what you're doing with the house,' I told the woman, 'and the bungalow will be good for you.' Her son told me afterwards that she was selling their house – to buy a bungalow. She squealed with delight when I told her that her husband was saying he'd met up with her father, 'Old Jack'. That's how her father had been known.

A good morning's work over, I went home to sleep it all off. Reconnecting people with those who have passed over can be an exhausting task, but judging by the smiles on their faces as they leave, it's well worth it.

CHAPTER 5

Seeing is believing

MY mediumship, my gift, began when I was a child and I have had many amazing psychic experiences since. There were many times during my psychic development, however, when I doubted what I was doing. On one of these occasions I remember saying to the spirit world, 'I don't want to do this, I really don't want to. You're going to have to prove to me beyond doubt that you really exist if you want me to go on.' That night I had to stand up on a platform and give messages to people, and the spirits came through and passed on the most incredible information to people who were really hurting. And I could see how that changed their lives. It changed mine too – I had to carry on.

Later, as I mentioned previously, I took part in some scientific tests conducted by Glasgow University, including more than one in which I was not even allowed to see the audience. The results were over 90 per cent accurate, even when I couldn't see the people I was passing information to or hear their responses to what I was saying. That gave me a lot more confidence – trust is probably a better word – in what I was doing. Now I know my gift has been well and truly proven and the important thing for me is to help people who are grieving for a loved one.

Most of it is not about psychic phenomena but about healing. Spirits only make things happen to get our attention. Once they have that attention, their aim is usually to give us a message, a positive message which includes assurances that they are not suffering, that they are free, that they are healed and in a better place than we are. If we all only knew that, we would be helped through the grieving process.

It's natural to feel sad when we lose someone, because we will miss them. On the other side, of course, there is a great celebration as they arrive 'home' and everyone is delighted to see them again. When we depart our physical body, the first thing that happens to us is that we are greeted by our loved ones who are already in the spirit world. Then we adjust back to our spirit selves. This is the state that we were in before we arrived here. Have you never wondered why babies cry when they come into this world? This earthly experience is one of the most difficult states that we will ever have to come through. When people talk to me about heaven and hell I tell them that there is only one place where both can be experienced (especially hell!), and that is in this human life.

Some people experience hell if they have to go through a separation or a divorce. Others are in living hells because they are trying to come off drugs or alcohol or deal with some other addiction. But all of these things relate only to our human life. As spirit beings, we are free of these emotional and physical pains. The sad thing is that we so often believe our human existence is all that there is. If we only realized how tiny our human existence is compared to our spiritual existence, we would be less inclined to fear this life. That little word 'fear' is what causes all of our hell. More people fall ill with cancer or other diseases through fear than any-thing else. A friend of mine who smoked was told by her spiritual teacher, 'If you're going to smoke, don't worry. The worry will kill you more quickly than the smoking.'

Part of what my work does is to teach people that they cannot die. As I often say, we cannot die for the life of us. And when we leave this world, everyone we have bonded with and loved will still be connected to us. We actually never lose anything or anyone we have loved. It doesn't matter whether it is a lover, a son, a mother, a dog or an unborn baby, if we have loved and felt love, we will retain that connection. Knowing this takes away the fear of life – and death. I have absolutely no fear of death, and having no fear of death automatically means that you have no fear of life either.

You have no idea what a reward that is for me, greater than any satisfaction money or possessions could ever bring. It leads to the realization that everything is happening because it should. Often we take the bad things that happen to us in life personally and say that someone must be to blame for them. And yet they're just what is supposed to happen. They are opportunities for us to learn. Some people think that if they have a child that is born with a disability they are being punished. They don't look at it from the point of view that they are being given a chance to love in a special way. People blame God, but God gives us opportunities, not punishments. I'm afraid it's people themselves who do the damage. In this human state we behave quite badly at times. But it's easier to blame God than to take responsibility for our own actions.

We need to learn that blaming and fighting and acting in a negative way just create more blame and fighting and negativity. And what's the point? It's all about greed and materialism, that's all. For some strange reason, most of us want to live on this little planet for as long as we can and have as much of it as we can. How foolish that seems when you realize that this world is the lowest realm of spirit you can live in and that in harming another, you harm yourself. In taking from someone what's not yours, you are really taking from yourself. There is a divine law called karma, and that word just means 'action'. So your actions have an effect.

If they are intended to harm someone, you will bring harm back to yourself in some way. If, however, you help people and love them, that same assistance and love will come back to you. It is one of the simplest teachings in the world: love one another.

You might wonder what this has to do with life after death. But all life is connected. This life, the next life, it's the same life, just an extension of it. So, by learning in this life we are preparing ourselves for what is to come.

Knowing that life goes on immediately connects you to the people you've lost, because they are still living too. The only thing that stops you getting to them or being able to see them, touch them and hold them is the fact that they are in a much finer state of vibration.

When my spirit teachers began teaching me about vibrational energy I didn't know what they were on about at first. Then it was shown to me that our physical bodies vibrate at a very slow rate. Think of your heartbeat for a moment. The spirit world, however, vibrates at a rate so fast that we cannot even sense it. In order to even begin to do so, we have to be in a state of mind – extremely anxious, for example – when our hearts are beating faster. This is why a lot of people have psychic experiences when they are anxious. Now I'm not advocating anxiety as a method of contacting loved ones on the other side. What I am saying is that we may find it difficult to sense our loved ones because our rate of vibration is not quick enough and they may find it difficult to slow down enough to reach us.

Mediums like me enable spirits to make contact with us by transforming energy from high to low frequency. In a way, this is no different from how a radio works. There are sound waves out there that we cannot pick up through our ears, and therefore we need some kind of receiver to adjust the vibration and bring it to our level. Mediums are rather like radio sets.

There will be times in your own life, however, when your loved ones will be able to come through to you directly. Some people have dreams of people that have died. Others sense that they are being watched. We all have a sixth sense that we use to pick up things in this way. You don't have to be a medium to employ it. It's that instinct, your sense of knowing something you have no reason to. We all have that inner power, but the problem is that we don't use it often enough, usually because we feel ridiculous and our rational mind dismisses it. But I can tell you that that inner instinct is something that more and more people are developing.

*****

After I had delivered these ideas to an audience of 'thinkers' in Greece, I submitted myself for questioning on any aspect of what I do and what I believe. One man asked me about prophecies that had been made in the past, in particular about the 'Golden Age' that has been promised, a time of peace and enlightenment. When would this happen? I told him that many considered it had already begun. It was prophesied to follow turbulent times of war and natural disasters and we have certainly had those in abundance. But I must point out that golden ages and times of peace and enlightenment do not belong to the physical world. This is not that kind of realm. It is through all the difficult things that happen here that we begin to learn to enlighten ourselves in preparation for a golden age in the next world. What is happening here is just a small part of spiritual evolution, a preparatory part. But we learn through the struggles in this life and we take that knowledge with us when we go back to our true home.

A woman then asked me how life in the next world would be for someone who was born into this world with a mental disability. I explained that this would not go with them into the next. It's all about consciousness, and the best way I can explain that is to ask you to imagine a rough diamond, an uncut stone, from which you hope to make a most beautiful multifaceted clear stone. Consciousness is like that and with each physical experience we chop at the rough stone and take it towards perfection. And in order to do so, to become completely enlightened, we need to experience everything. So a person with a mental illness – be it man, woman or child – would have chosen to come into this life with that disability to experience it and learn from it. Many cultures treat such people as very special because of the burden they have chosen to carry here.

I was asked next what happens to people who are 'bad' in this life. My answer is that it depends on what you consider a good or bad person. Who knows what's inside them, how pure they really are? You might be referring to a person who is quite pure but has just done something bad. And ultimately, that person's judge will be themselves. Take, for example, a person who has killed someone. When they go to the spirit world they are going to have to see how that affected so many people – the victim's mother, father, lover, friends, even the people who found the body. It will be a weight on their conscience, but it will not be the only thing that they have done in this life, so it will be a matter of weighing up the whole life and evaluating it.

To a lady who asked how she could connect with the spirit world I said we can all connect with it once we realize that we are spirits inside human bodies. The moment we are aware of that, we will make that connection. Here we often use language to lie to each other. In the spirit world, we can't. That world is so uncomplicated and the more we connect to it, the less complicated we become and the easier our connection to the other side becomes.

*****

Most of the questions I was asked that day were to do with spirituality. I have found that this develops out of compassion. And out of compassion comes wisdom. We need both these virtues to develop spiritually in this life. And the more we grow spiritually, the more we reach out to all life and the more 'paranormal' things just happen naturally to us. So many people assume that great rituals or practices have to be performed in order to develop spiritually, but that's not the case.

I hope that people in the world just now are starting to wake up, that their spirits are starting to wake up, because it's only when we think spiritually that we will in fact bring some kind of order back to this world. I hope that the messages that I bring through to people teach them not only about their own relatives but that the afterlife is open to all of us – even those who don't believe. Belief belongs to this world too.

Whatever you believe, your life force is going to go on to somewhere. Your consciousness already travels away from the body when you are asleep. If only you knew what you were doing while you were asleep – and I mean spiritually. You are going 'home' each night.

So, if ever you are finding things difficult to deal with, just remember that there's much more to life than the here-and-now and that everything is happening because it should. Life is a great opportunity.

CHAPTER 6

Take the love...

MEDIUMSHIP gets me around the globe far more than hairdressing ever did. It's hard to imagine two places less alike than Athens and Llandudno, but within two weeks of my extraordinary Greek odyssey I was sitting in a delightful country garden sipping tea with friends just five miles outside this charming Welsh resort.

Llandudno is a perfectly preserved Victorian seaside resort set on a spectacular half-moon of a bay. Armed with an ice-cream cone, I took in the traditional Punch and Judy show on the prom near the pier head. Watching Mr Punch squawking half-intelligible messages at an enthralled audience, all alone on his little stage, I thought, 'That's me tonight!'

I had been booked into a beautiful country house of a hotel just five miles inland and I spent a sunny afternoon before the event relaxing in the private garden of my room.

I'm often asked how I prepare for an event. Do I have some kind of physical or mental workout routine, a kind of psychic warm-up that I go through to get myself ready for the rigours of a three-hour session in front of an expectant audience who have given up their time and paid for seats at an evening of mediumship? The truth is that I don't have or want such preparation. If I thought about how I was going to spend my evening I would end up freaking out! Just imagine: three hours alone on stage in front of 1,000 people with no script and not a clue about what – if anything – is going to take place…

Every event is absolutely unique and I really don't know what's going to happen any more than the audience does. It's a real act of faith and I cope with it by putting it out of my mind until it's time to go on stage. Beforehand I just relax and try and make sure I'm rested, fit and ready for whatever fate has in store for me. After all, my name may be on the bill, but it's not my show. The word 'medium' comes from the same root as 'media'. I'm a messenger, a carrier of messages.

At Llandudno I got to the smart new seafront theatre, the Venue Cymru, half an hour before going on stage.

The audience was already filing into the auditorium – over 1,000 people of all ages. I reckoned there were slightly more women than men, but not by much.

After the dramas of Greece it was wonderful to have a fun evening on the North Wales coast. Yes, I know we were dealing with the spirits of people who had departed this life and left behind this capacity audience of grieving relatives and friends. But that night they were mostly happy spirits – though for the first few minutes they seemed like a shy lot and I had to chat away before one of them would come through. When he did, he turned out to be a fellow who gave us all plenty of laughs. He had passed unexpectedly, leaving rather a lot of unfinished business, but he talked of meeting her mother on the other side, his daughter's forthcoming birthday and a Mick he knew would be in the pub. He directed me to his wife and gave her plenty of proof that he was indeed there, including bragging about his earthly good looks and the handsome shock of dark hair that had always been his pride and joy. When I told her some papers had arrived at their home which she had to sign, she said, 'Yes, that's true.' Finally her husband wanted her to know that the results of some medical tests she was going to have to take (she confirmed that she already had an appointment) were going to be fine, which must have been a great relief to her.

The spirits reminded more than one member of the audience of favourite songs they had shared, including Whitney Houston's 'I Will Always Love You' – that drew a few tears – and 'Danny Boy'.

One lady was transported back to the Côte d'Azur and squealed in delight when a man who had left her earthly life recalled happy memories of their visits to Monte Carlo, and another was reminded of wonderful times on the Isle of Man but a difficult moment when a water bed burst! Once they had started, the spirits could have kept me going all night.

I hope that all those who received messages also heeded what I often pass on in conclusion: 'Take the love.' That sums up what the spirits have to offer: comfort.

Imagine, for example, what it must be like to witness first-hand the death of one of your family and know there is nothing that you can do to stop it. That must be a living hell.

At the end of December 2006 I was asked to give a sitting to a lady named Jayne Charles at a Spiritualist church in London. I hadn't known that she would be bringing anyone with her, so I was quite surprised when a woman in her fifties walked into the little sitting room with a young man I would say was in his early twenties.

This wasn't a problem, just unexpected.

I could tell by looking at the couple that they had recently suffered a loss. Just the way they walked – in a very tense way, holding themselves as though they were suffering from pains in their stomachs, with their heads seeming to rest on their chests – told me how deflated they were.

As usual I welcomed them into the room and began to explain what might or might not happen during their sitting. As I pulled over a second chair for the young man and looked into his eyes for a moment, I felt my own stomach react as though a huge stone had just fallen through it. At once I knew that this was his feeling, not mine. Often when I am giving sittings, people's feelings when they walk in the door transfer to me for a while. I am very used to this, but this time it was a really terrible feeling. It gave me a good indication of the depth of despair this young man was suffering.

The sitting began with two people coming through at once. It was difficult to separate them at first, but Jayne said that she recognized both. The main communicator was a young woman who told me that her name was Gill. The second person was an older woman whom I felt was Jayne's mother. But I felt that she was only there to help the younger woman to communicate her message.

As I spoke, I found myself turning towards to the young man and addressing him more than I did Jayne. He never gave me any direct eye contact at first and just kept his chin resting on his chest. Gill mentioned the word 'brother' and I felt that this was her brother in front of me. As I said this, he lifted his head and looked at me. At once I felt the huge weight hit my gut again and I silently asked Gill to help him. So many times in my mediumship I have sent out thoughts like this to the spirit world and so many times they have come back with something important that has brought forth an immediate reaction.

This time Gill's response was: 'It wasn't your fault, John!' The words seemed to pass through my mind and out of my mouth before I could even consider what was being said.

When he heard this, the young man's eyes bulged out of his head and tears welled up and began to pour down his face as if someone just turned on two great taps.

Jayne took his hand and also started crying. By now I had realized that this was mother and son and Gill was Jayne's daughter on the other side trying to help her brother, who was obviously there because he felt some-how responsible for her death.

When people become very emotional during sittings, I try not to become affected by it. It is much more pro-ductive for me to tune in harder and get on with trying to get more information for them. But this time I had to drop my head and blink back tears as I tried to carry on with the message.

As I concentrated on Gill I could see her in a small red car driving at high speed into a lamp-post. I could also see her brother and a small group of other people his age running and screaming. John was trying to pull the door of the car open. At that point the vision ended.

I didn't report to my sitters what I had seen, but instead asked for more help from the spirit world.

Gill told me that there wasn't anything her brother could have done. She said that she had found herself standing on the pavement looking at the scene and hadn't been able to understand what everyone was doing screaming and fussing around her car. By this I knew that she had already gone at that point and that she hadn't even felt a thing. The next thing she knew, she told me, was that her nana, as she called her, was standing with her somewhere else and she was OK.

I passed this message back to John and Jayne, and midway through it I heard Gill say, 'I know what he wants to do with his arm!' I interrupted what I was saying to repeat what she had told me, as it seemed important to her to prove that she was still aware of what was going on in John's life. So often spirits do this to confirm to their loved ones that their consciousness is still in touch with them.

Mother and son looked at each other and for the first time they smiled, first at each other and then at me.

I continued to pass on this new train of thought coming through from Gill. 'I think it's stupid, but he'll do it anyway!' came next.

This time there was a laugh from John and Jayne. They said that was exactly the way Gill would have spoken and also what they would have expected her to say about John's wish to have her name tattooed on his arm!

Gill gave me more details of things her brother had done and was thinking of doing since her untimely passing, all of which were now accepted by two smiling people. Tears and laughter were coming together, especially when Gill reminded John about him burying her pet hamster when he was only 12, only to discover shortly afterwards, when Gill dug the creature up, that it was only hibernating. Jayne reassured me that it had been wrapped in one of John's T-shirts and put in a box that was probably large enough to have contained enough air to have kept it alive during its momentary burial.

Gill's message to her mother and brother lasted only about 45 minutes, but in that short time she seemed to change her brother's feelings about her death. I also noticed that the terrible feeling in my stomach had dissipated and both my sitters were laughing a lot and looking much more relaxed than they had when they arrived.

Jayne explained to me that when she had got a chance to have a private sitting, she felt she had to bring her son, as he had been having terrible nightmares about his sister's death. As I had seen, he had been standing with his friends at the end of the street where they lived when his sister's car had smashed into a wall 100 yards from their home. After that, he had become so depressed at the thought of not being able to save his sister that he had stopped his studies. Jayne told me that she hadn't seen him smile since the accident and he was becoming reclusive. Other than wanting to go out and have a tattoo done in Gill's memory, he hadn't shown any interest in leaving his home. He was so terrified that he might have to go past the place where Gill had died, which Jayne said was now just a mass of wilted flowers.

I have never heard the outcome of this sitting, but I do feel that, if nothing else, John and Jayne felt that they had a conversation with Gill that day – a conversation where the young lady in the spirit world tried to take away their deepest fears about her death. She wanted to see her brother start to live again. And she wanted him to know that no matter what he thought or how he tortured his mind, she was now safe in the spirit world and still watching over him and still very much connected to all of her family. My deepest wish is that it made a change to a young man's life, a change that would see him get back to his studies and make his sister proud of him.

*****

Spirits who make the effort to come through a medium like myself at demonstrations for, say several hundred people, always have a purpose in doing so. Most come back to help the grieving, as Gill did, but some do it because when they died they left unfinished business, so when I am asked if I come across spirits who would rather be here than there, the answer is sometimes 'Yes.' They have a kind of anxiety about the person or persons left behind, a need to help them.

Of course, someone might well say, 'Well, my mother died very suddenly and she hasn't come back to help me cope with all she left behind. Why is that?' The answer is, every person differs and so does every spirit. We are dealing here with so many different kinds of grief, so many completely different reactions, on both sides, that it is foolish to generalize. Even two people who come along for a private sitting will usually have different reactions to what they hear. A mother might want to hear from her son, for example, and if he comes through it will help her considerably to cope with grief and she will go away feeling lighter and happier. Her husband, on the other hand, may feel slightly redundant because his wife isn't desperately dependent on him any more. So he is very switched-off to the idea of their son coming through via me. 'Why you?' he will say. I have to be very aware of this kind of situation when I am communicating.

That happened recently with a woman called Mandy who was sent to me by a friend. After her daughter had given sound evidence to her she turned to her husband and said, 'It's her, it's got to be her. Who else would know the things Gordon is passing on?' But the man didn't want to be convinced, and snapped, 'No, I'm not buying into this. I need to find out how much he knows about us.' Of course, I didn't have a clue who they were or what their story was, but I recognized his need to establish that his daughter would not confide in a complete stranger.

I never heard from them again and don't know whether the man finally accepted the message I had delivered or not. I hope that when he and his wife listened to the tape together later, his feelings changed. But the thing is that their reactions were so different. The man was upset, very upset, and he got more and more so as what came through proved evidential. He would have gone away happier, I am sure, if nothing had come through. I have to allow for situations like that.

*****

A quite common reason why spirits who have passed suddenly want to communicate is to reassure their loved ones as to the nature of their death. At one public gathering, a spirit was desperate to come through and directed me to two ladies at the back of the hall.

'He's telling me you are sisters and that he's your brother,' I told them.

Though clearly in a state of some distress, they nodded in agreement.

'He was a heroin addict and you think he took his own life, but he wants you to know that wasn't so. He says he'd managed to kick the habit for a while but when he went back on the drug he took a hit that was impure or just too strong. He wants you to know it was not his intention to die.'

Afterwards one of them approached me and expressed her gratitude for the message. She said it had taken a weight off the family's minds, for they believed that their brother was in purgatory – 'stuck somewhere', as she put it. So many people believe that if you do the wrong thing in this life you will have a dreadful afterlife, and it's wonderful when a message from spirit relieves a grieving person of that additional distress.

*****

While I was in Llandudno, Carole Smith from Meols in the Wirral came to see me. She was accompanied by a particularly talkative spirit, a young woman who also had an older woman with her.

'I don't know who this young lady is, but it's apparent that you have a very strong bond with her,' I told Carole.

I felt a sharp intake of breath, indicating that the

woman went quite suddenly. 'I have my nan here with me,' she was saying. 'Tell Mum I'm with Grandma.'

That was only the start. This lady had so much to tell me. I sensed that there had been more than the usual amount of sadness associated with her passing. She had made many plans for her life but she had also been aware of a serious health problem that might have made those plans unfeasible and had been prepared to die, which had made things easier for her than for those she had left behind.

There were family connections in both the Liverpool and Chester areas, and she was sending love to several young children, showing me a beautiful picture and mentioning a hip operation. She referred to a photograph that was very special to Carole and others, and said she was at a birthday party very recently. 'John' was being written up on what I sometimes refer to as the spiritual blackboard and 'Jean is here with me,' she was adding.

How this spirit loved to talk – and she obviously had a great sense of humour, because her message was laced with wit, especially when mentioning her 'beautiful hair'. She took me to an area with grass and trees – not a domestic garden – where, she said, she and Carole had a favourite walk, and she showed me daffodils and a dog that she was insistent I mentioned.

Then, showing me a passport, she took me abroad and mentioned memories of a villa where lots of other photographs had been taken. These photos were now in a container crammed with memorabilia, something made with shells. Others had been mounted in a montage that she greatly appreciated.

Playfully, she put a hat of some sort on my head and then she handed me a ring that was obviously significant. September, she said, was important for memories. A grandfather came forward – William, or Billy, as he was known. The name 'Jack' was also called out, and then 'Paul'. Someone else, she noticed, was losing his hair, someone who had to wear a suit for work. Carole, she said, had her glasses. A radio tuned to a music station was playing. She made me count to ten, the tenth month: October. A Wendy was mentioned, or was it Wednesday? The information was flowing too fast for me to get all of it accurately. She was showing me a beautiful card. 'You've kept the card,' she was saying. And then she switched to a special dinner. 'I'll be there with you,' she wanted Carole to know.

'Tell my Mum I love her,' she concluded. 'Tell her I'm free now. Look at the things I can do now!' And with that she was gone.

Afterwards Carole told me that she had received what she had set out to get on her journey to Llandudno – a message from her daughter Julie, who had been born with spina bifida and hydrocephalus and been confined to a wheelchair up to her death, aged 32, in 1999. Despite her serious physical limitations Julie had always been a bright, upbeat person who was full of fun and had seen the best in people – exactly the impression I had formed as I had received her message.

Here's the rest of what Carole had to say:

It was absolutely amazing. Julie's personality really shone through. Gordon kept giggling and laughing just as she would have done. The photograph she talked about was taken eight years earlier to the day. All the members of the family have copies of it in their homes.

It was Jessie, the mother of my husband Rob, who was waiting for Julie. They were always close. Julie loved her nephews and nieces and mentioned Jack, who was born after she died. It's great that she still knows about them all. I had a hip operation last year. I still tell Julie everything that is happening in the family. It was my granddaughter Ruby's fourth birthday party last weekend and it's Rob's birthday this week – I've organized a family dinner to celebrate it.

It's wonderful news that she's standing tall and looks beautiful. She liked to look nice and loved her long hair.

Julie was very funny and she did like to have a laugh, especially with her brother Paul. They were so close. He's a solicitor, so has to wear suits. John was my dad's brother and Jean is Rob's sister. She passed suddenly in the night a year ago. Julie's sister Natalie has a birthday and a wedding anniversary in October.

I used to walk Julie every day to a small park near our house with Tammy our dog and we would admire the gardens on the way. Julie especially loved daffodils.

We went to Florida in 1997 and stayed in a villa. Julie loved it. The cap was from DisneyWorld – somewhere she had always wanted to go.

Carrie, Julie's sister, is getting married this year and we thought that playing Julie's favourite songs would be too sad, but Julie has now told her that she must play her music. On the day Carrie will be wearing the sapphire and diamond ring that Julie was given for her 21st birthday.

Her birthday was 26 September. Both her granddads were called Bill. I keep special bits [of memorabilia] in a box covered with shells, including her glasses.

Wendy is a friend of mine who is with me here in Llandudno today – and it's a Wednesday.

Tell Julie I love her too.

Clearly mother and daughter have fond memories of each other and that encounter alone was enough to leave me with happy memories of that particular visit to North Wales, where I know that some of the spirit messages changed some lives for the better.

CHAPTER 7

Talking to the
'well-connected'

I was asked by a friend if I would give a sitting to a lady he knew who was in great need.

When I entered her house in the centre of London, I realized that this was the home of a person of means, and yet the back sitting room I was led into was less grand and had a more lived-in feel.

After the usual introductions and spelling out how a private sitting with a medium might work, we got underway.

Almost at once the lady's brother came through. 'I have your brother here,' I said. 'He died quite recently.' She nodded in agreement.

'He's telling me that he was in the country with other people when he died and that he had dogs around him. You are under the impression that he died in hospital, but he actually passed over before they even got him into the ambulance – while they were trying to revive him, in fact.'

Now she showed surprise because, she explained, she had always believed that his death had taken place in hospital, but her brother was insistent that he had died where he fell.

'If you don't believe him, ask the doctor,' I said.

The point of this is that the lady had been torturing herself with thoughts of 'Could we have done any-thing?' but her brother was aware of that and wanted her to know that there was absolutely nothing anyone could have done.

'He also says, "Tell my sister there was no need to put the photographs away."'

At that, she looked at me and said, 'Oh, my God!'

'He also says that there was a bust of him and some-body stuck a cigarette in its mouth and a drink under its chin when he passed. It was a laugh, although he was proud of having given up a big smoking habit.'

'Nobody outside a select few of us knows that,' said the lady, amazed. 'The bust is in his own home, which I am visiting tomorrow, in fact.'

And so it went on. 'He says he bought you a dog

named Lady...'

'He did – for my birthday when I was young.'

'He mentions a Mini and Sloane Street, and this is a memory which goes back some time.'

She confirmed that these memories were special to her and her brother.

At one point I mimicked smoking a cigarette with one hand and pushing my other hand through my hair.

'That's his exact pose,' she said. 'He had long hair and he used to do that when he was smoking.'

Somewhere in myself I had the feeling that I should know who this man was. There was something very familiar about the whole thing, yet the way he gave information to his sister suggested that he wanted to retain some anonymity. In such cases I have to respect that. It doesn't matter to me whom I see – whether they come from the highest of backgrounds or the lowest. This gracious lady was obviously from the first, but, more importantly, I could see that a joy had come into her eyes – a joy that had been absent when I had first met her.

It is clear to me now that the reason photographs had been removed from her sitting room was because her brother was instantly recognizable and she did not want that to influence her sitting – and she was right.

My job that day was not to impress my sitter, nor be impressed by who she was or her brother was, but to help heal the pain she was going through – the pain of losing someone so close. She also needed to hear her brother tell her that she couldn't have done anything to save him. The thought that there might have been something she could have done had been such a heavy burden that it had made her ill both mentally and physically – so much so that she had ended up consulting a medium to try and find peace.

It must have been two weeks after the sitting that I received a call from her. She sounded jubilant, her voice brimming with hope and excitement like that of someone who has just been told they have won the lottery.

She couldn't wait to tell me that after many days considering all that had happened at our meeting, she had taken it upon herself to contact the doctor who had dealt with her brother on his arrival at the hospital. She had asked him straight out if her brother had been alive when he arrived and if the medical staff had made efforts to resuscitate him. The doctor was astounded by her questioning and asked why she wanted such information now. But eventually he gave in and told her that nothing could have been done to help her brother and he was indeed dead on arrival. He asked her why she suspected that might be the case, but she didn't tell him. She wanted to keep to herself the fact that her brother had told her through a medium. But she also wanted to let me know that she was in no doubt that she had spoken to her brother that day and that he had come to help her. Also, her own health had improved remarkably since the sitting and all of her friends and family were amazed at her recovery.

I was so pleased to hear this, as it confirmed to me yet again that spirits' main intention in making contact with their loved ones is to heal them and help them back to life. And, may I add, it doesn't matter which level of society you live on. Neither riches nor fame can prevent suffering touching our lives.

*****

Talking of fame – and I have met some very famous people on my travels, mostly through mediumship – one person I always wanted to meet was the great actress, singer, dancer and author, Shirley MacLaine. This was not only because I enjoyed her films like *Sweet Charity* and *Terms of Endearment*, to name just a couple, but also because I enjoyed her books and felt strangely drawn to her as a person.

Back in 1995 I was asked to give a demonstration of mediumship in Gibraltar. It was the first time I had ever worked in a large theatre; usually I demonstrated in Spiritualist churches or small halls around the UK. I still remember how frightened I was when I was standing backstage, smoking a cigarette out of the open window of my small dressing room.

Looking out of that window in a state of shock, I noticed only one thing: a tree that was bare of leaves – bare of anything other than one orange hanging from the highest branch. There was something about the sight that made me feel strange inside. Then I heard a voice inside my head speaking to me. It said, 'To reach the fruit of the tree, you have to go out on a limb.'

I don't know why, but hearing that phrase, which I had never heard before, made me feel connected to a source much greater than myself. I felt that I was going out on a limb, yet I also felt safe – safer than I had ever felt as a medium before. It was like being wrapped in a warm blanket by an unseen force that was there to protect and guide me.

After this amazing experience all I remember about

that night was that I worked with a confidence that was new to me, and messages came through for very many people with real accuracy and relevance.

It wasn't until I got home that a friend of mine gave me a copy of a book by Shirley MacLaine called *Out on a Limb*. I remember being fascinated and dying to read it. I wanted to know if it could shed any light on the strange way I had felt when I was working in Gibraltar. I enjoyed reading the book, as it helped me to understand more about synchronicity and started me on a very different journey. I also experienced a similar thing to the moment with the fruit tree when reading the start of the book. 'Malibu beach at sunset,' it said, 'always makes me think that there's got to be more to life than this.' It's nothing profound, is it? Yet reading it I felt that I was there with Shirley – or at least I had a strange sense that I would somehow end up on Malibu beach at sunset. It is difficult to explain, but it was as if I was seeing a vision of the future. However, as with all the other visions of future events I have ever had, it was difficult to make sense of it until it actually happened.

Now here is where it gets even stranger. I was due to work in Las Vegas in May 2007 and had decided that I would take a few extra days to relax and have a bit of a holiday. Just before I was due to fly out, a friend of mine asked me to go stay with her in Los Angeles for a couple of days. She lived by the ocean and thought it would be nicer for Jim and me to be there than in the desert of Nevada, more nurturing. Also, we both wanted some time to talk about mediumship and how it might work well on a TV programme.

When we arrived in LA she collected us and we set off for her home overlooking the ocean. What dawned on me on the way was that we were heading out of LA, leaving the Hollywood Hills sign in the distance, towards Malibu. I was actually going to be on Malibu beach at sunset – a dream realized after 12 years.

Walking on that beach that evening, I found it was just as Shirley MacLaine had described it. There was a magic in the way the sea met the land and the colours of the mystical sunset blended with the mountains. Part of me felt small by comparison, yet I also felt connected to the great source that had created such amazing beauty. I really understood what Miss MacLaine had meant, and yet something was missing – I had always thought I would meet Shirley MacLaine herself if I ever got there!

Yet even as I sent out that thought, there was a re-assuring voice telling me, 'All is as it should be.' I seemed to know that all was well and I remember thinking that if Shirley were here somewhere she would somehow find me. I gave that thought to the ocean, went back to my friend's beautiful home overlooking the Pacific Ocean and slept as I had not slept in years.

I woke early the following morning feeling good. I felt as though something was about to happen, only I had no idea what it was going to be.

After breakfast Jim and I accompanied my friend to her local hair salon in Malibu, where she was doing some filming. Both of us are comfortable in salons, having worked as hairdressers for many years.

Whilst I was in the salon I got chatting to the receptionist, a very nice woman, who told me that her family originated in Scotland. No sooner had she said this than I felt her father come through. He told me that he came from Aberdeen and began to bring through a message that the lady needed to hear at that time. She was so pleased to hear from him, quite overwhelmed in fact, and when I had finished she said she would like to do something for me. Just joking, I told her not to bother unless she could materialize Shirley MacLaine. But then it was my turn to be shocked when she said, 'I think I can do that. Give me a minute.'

At first I thought she was joking with me the same way that I was with her, but moments later she told me that Miss MacLaine was on her way and would love to meet me! It's an old cliché, but my jaw did drop.

Forty minutes later the door of the beautifully appointed salon opened and in walked the Oscar-winning actress. I remember thinking how ordinary she looked dressed in trousers, T-shirt and sweater – ordinary, that is, until I looked into her eyes. If the eyes are truly the windows of the soul, then these amazing sparkling eyes seemed to show a soul that was as vast as the ocean I had looked at the previous evening.

I wouldn't say that I was as much starstruck as gob-smacked. Shirley took over at once, whisking us out of the salon and into a nearby restaurant, where we immediately began to talk about spiritual matters. She was very interested in them, but it was so refreshing to realize how down-to-earth she was as well, and how interested in life on all levels. For once in my life I wanted to shut up and listen rather than pitch in my tuppence worth. Shirley's knowledge of spiritual matters is vast and it was just fascinating to absorb what she was giving off. I don't remember what she ate; it didn't seem important, considering. There was something so electric about the moment, so otherworldly, it was as if we were floating above our seats.

I knew Shirley was very comfortable with all things spiritual, as she had had many fantastic life experiences in the field. This meant that I didn't have to explain myself as I usually do when speaking to celebrities. She was happy talking to us about her thoughts on consciousness, life after death and the future of the planet. She seemed to be someone who had understood her spiritual path and whose mind had expanded because of it.

After lunch I agreed to do a private sitting for her. The only place we could go to do it was the hair salon, but when we got back there all the chairs were full. Then someone suggested the stock cupboard! I had no problems with this, but I didn't feel it a fitting venue for a Hollywood legend. Shirley, though, just shrugged her shoulders and flashed that famous smile at me as she stretched out her hand and led me into the cupboard, where we sat down together on the many boxes of hair products.

Shirley's sitting was easy for me, as she was used to sitting with people like me. By that I mean that it was not evidence she was looking for. She already knew there was life after death and just wanted to know how her loved ones on the other side felt about certain things in her life. It reminded me of when I met William Roache from *Coronation Street*. He, too, had no need of evidence; he just treated the occasion like a phone call – if anyone had anything to say they would come to the phone.

Meeting Shirley MacLaine was like meeting an old friend. After I had got over who she was in this physical life – and that was made much easier by the ordinary way she behaved – it was like reconnecting with someone I already knew. I didn't make it happen, but it was always going to. And I just accept such things, as does Shirley.

There is something very uplifting about realizing that the things that happen in life are meant to happen. It gives me a feeling that no matter what befalls us, somewhere inside us, we know it was meant. And whether the events are 'good' or 'bad', we want to experience them in order to learn something. They are not punishment or reward, but are there to teach us.

One experience I have had a lot in recent years is that of meeting famous people. I have given private sittings to many of them. But, like my old friend Albert Best, who was a very honourable medium, I see most of them just as people who come to me because they have a need, like all people who come for help from the spirit world. There are so many that I could write about only because of their fame or power, but that would feel as though I was betraying them.

The difference with Miss MacLaine, as I said to her at the end of our sitting, was how funny it was, with all the synchronicity and finally finding ourselves crushed together in a small cupboard. How less grand could it be?! She told me that I should put it in my next book, so here it is. And the meeting was indeed a life-changing message for me.

*****

I never had the pleasure of meeting Ross Davidson, who played nurse Andy O'Brien in *EastEnders*, in person, but I was happy to relay a message to his widow Barbara not long after he died in 2006. I was unaware of her association with the popular actor when we met, but when a big smiley Scotsman came through, it was obvious to me that he was no shrinking violet. When I asked for evidence, he gave me two numbers to throw at Barbara – the 16th and the 25th. 'My husband was born on 25 August and he died on 16 October,' she said, 'so that's Ross.'

Meanwhile he was telling me he had died of a serious head illness at home after a spell in hospital where he remembers his children coming one by one to visit him.

'He died of brain cancer,' Barbara confirmed.

He also talked of an area not far from Glasgow Zoo, which turned out to be where his mother lived. He mentioned that Barbara wore his ring on a chain around her neck. And there was plenty more where that came from which was personal to the couple, who had been married for just 18 months.

The odd thing about this sitting was that Ross was telling me Barbara had brought his brother to the sitting, but there were only two of us – plus the spirit, of course – in the room. I asked her about this.

'No, he's not here,' she replied.

'Ross is telling me he is,' I said.

It turned out that his brother had arrived too late for the start of the sitting and was waiting for her in an outer room.

*****

I remember thinking about celebrities and people who find themselves in the public eye the evening after meeting

Shirley MacLaine. Ironically, I was sitting on Malibu beach at sunset at the time. In a place like this celebs go almost unnoticed. People just pass by contemplating life, their life, no matter who they are. And everybody has ups and downs in this life. Each of us is only human, after all, and our downs usually make us more aware of that humanity. It's then that we feel the weight of this world. We can all be made to feel limited and small and all that we have achieved can be made to feel like nothing. 'People are just people,' I thought, 'trying to get on with life, trying to find their individuality and define it through whatever is happening in their life at that moment.'

When the famous aren't on TV, in films or on the covers of magazines, they too are trying to work out their lives, wondering what it's all about and often realizing that in their individuality they are only human. 'How many people,' I wondered, 'famous or otherwise, on this beach are aware that we are all connected, all part of the same source which is greater than any individual and yet part of them at the same time?'

It was about then that I walked back to the restaurant where Jim and my friend were waiting. I was standing outside it for a moment just to take in another moment of Malibu beach at sunset and have a last cigarette when a young couple approached me. The young man, very handsome and athletic-looking, asked me if he could have a cigarette. I was offering him the pack when the young lady, who was holding on to his arm, asked if she could also have one. 'Of course,' I said.

The lady was wearing a hood and the way she was dressed wasn't particularly special, but as she lit her cigarette from my lighter she removed her hood and said, 'Doesn't this make you feel that there's got to be more to life than this?'

I looked at her face and thought, 'Don't I know you?'

It was the screen actress Daryl Hannah, just being herself, an ordinary person.

I replied, 'Yes, it's a magical place.'

CHAPTER 8

Living life with spirit

FLYING into Cape Town, I read in the airline magazine that the city had been voted one of the top places to see 'before you die'. We can't help bringing death into our everyday conversation, can we? Such and such is 'to die for' or something will only happen 'over my dead body'. But the message I was bringing to South Africa was that death is not the end of the road. When someone dies their body may be redundant but their spirit carries on. The 'Rainbow Nation' is a wonderful country and Cape Town, with its miles and miles of beautiful beaches, the fantastic Table Mountain and sprawling wine lands to the east is, OK, to die for. There's something for everyone: all the tourist sites you could want at the Victoria and Albert Waterfront, African penguins on the beach at Boulders and light-fingered pickpocket baboons on the road along the way to Cape Point lighthouse. Camps Bay is one of the sexiest beaches on Earth, with the Camps Bay kittens parading in their tangas and the bling-bling cowboys prowling the sidewalk coffee bars, bringing a touch of Miami South Beach to this very different continent.

But that's only one part of the rainbow. At Simon's Town's lovely Tibetan tearooms, where genuine prayer bowls are on offer with the superb vegetarian meals, I talked to an old-timer whose grandfather, according to the South African categorization of the times, was white and grandmother coloured. He told me about the old days: 'They'd poke a pencil into your hair. If it stayed there when your head was bent forward you would be classified as black or coloured. That would determine the course of the rest of your life – where you could stay, what jobs you could do, how much education you could get.'

In Langa, the oldest black township in Cape Town, 100 people would be crammed into a living space intended for 16. But now, although the dwellings look like jumbles of corrugated iron, inside they're neat and often packed with people seemingly happy to watch soaps on daytime TV.

I flew on to Johannesburg, where I met Denise

Maidment, a company director. For the ten years before her death her mother had been an integral part of her family unit, along with her husband and three sons.

Denise takes up the story:

Mum had always believed in the spirit world. She spoke to my granddad and gran every day of her life, though they had both passed years before. It was a subject that was regularly talked about in our house and always sparked colourful discussions.

While Mum believed in the afterlife, my husband disbelieved, the boys avoided the subject and I was terrified of the thought that someone dead could be standing next to me. The conversation usually ended with Mum saying, 'I will prove to you there is an afterlife and will come back and talk to you.' Rob would say, 'You just do that,' but I'd shiver at the thought and pleaded with her not to scare me.

In November 2004 she was taken ill and admitted to hospital. After several tests it was revealed she had stomach cancer and a huge tumour on her brain. The doctors ruled out treatment and gave us a time frame of about three months.

Mum was told and she took it really well, saying she'd had a great life and was ready to pass. Her only concern was that she wanted to go home because it was not fair to expect me to make the journey to the hospital every day – so typical of Mum.

My brothers and sisters were scattered around the world and we had not been together for 25 years. As sometimes happens in families, we had argued and fallen out with each other over the years, silly things had got in the way and distance was easy to blame for us not communicating too often. But Mum asked me to gather them all as she wanted to see us all together one more time and she said, 'Do it soon.'

I set about doing what she had asked me to do. It's hard to call your siblings and tell them your mother is dying and they need to get here quickly, but I did it and within a week every one had arranged flights and they were all arriving on the Friday morning.

Mum finally admitted she was in pain and morphine was prescribed. She did not want to take it, but I insisted. I was now the parent and she the child. I won and she took her medicine. This action was to haunt and torment me, no matter what anybody said.

Friday morning came and the clan gathered. Mum had her children with her for the first time in 25 years. The atmosphere was light-hearted and cheerful and Mum held court. I dutifully administered her morphine every four hours, always under protest, but I was determined she would not be in any pain. Then, while she was sleeping, the phone rang. It was the pharmacist. They had made a mistake with her scrip, and her morphine was too strong.

By now Mum was in bed and wasn't able to move or talk properly. She was seeing rainbows everywhere and talking about us children as if we were still all little ones. On Saturday the family sat around her bed, talking about our lives and hers, and sharing laughter and tears. There were her six children and the son-in-law she loved so much all together again. But Mum was in a coma caused by the morphine I had given her. She was unable to see her family whole again, a dream she had held close for so many years. And it was all my fault.

When she breathed her last I was sitting on the bed holding her hand and her family was showering her with love and releasing her. Without fuss she passed away, brave to the end.

The following days passed in a blur. My family scattered again and life gradually returned to normal.

But despite the assurances from the medical fraternity and her husband, Denise could not pick up where she had left off:

I researched the effects of morphine and convinced myself I had caused the coma – after all, I had forced her to take the medicine. I felt that I should have listened to her and that it was my fault that she never got to hear us talking on that Saturday.

Denise would have lived the rest of her life wracked with guilt had it not been for a series of strange chances.

She explains:

I advertise in a local magazine but never actually read it, as I'm too busy. However, the December issue was on my desk and for once I did read it, which was strange. In it I saw an advert for the Gordon Smith workshop in Johannesburg. I mentioned it to my husband and he said, 'Let's go!' which was another strange thing, considering his disbelief in the whole subject.

I booked and in February we went to see Gordon at a very busy seminar on a very thunder-filled afternoon. When he took to the stage, he wasn't what I was expecting at all. He was a real person, very mellow and with a sense of humour. He explained about the spirit world and what to expect from the demonstration. He also encouraged us to talk to him if we felt any message coming through was for us.

Then he moved to the side of the room we were sitting in and started to describe the spirit talking to him: 'A lady who passed recently, very quickly, but she was ready to go.'

'That has to be your mum,' my husband said. 'Put your hand up!'

I raised my hand to accept the message somewhat reluctantly, but then Gordon described Mum's death perfectly. She told us that she knew we were all there and had heard us talking. She said I was holding her hand and wanted me to know most of all that it was not my fault – she was ready to pass over. 'Thank you for looking after me for so long,' she added.

By this stage I was crying uncontrollably. I could only listen to Gordon's message and release all of my built-up emotions.

Gordon described the mints and false teeth Mum used to have in her pocket to scare the children as a joke, her wig-wearing picture that we used on her memorial notice and the people who were with her helping her to pass the message on. He told me about my upcoming trip to the UK to take her ashes back and most of all said Mum knew all about it because she had been with me when I had spoken to my sister on the phone a few days earlier. This thought would have freaked me out in the past, but when Gordon was telling me I felt a glow of warmth and comfort at the thought that Mum was still with us.

The messages became more relevant and meaningful as Gordon continued. He shared an intense feeling of love and gratitude that Mum was sending to us and finished with the words: 'She is saying she missed a birthday at Christmas but sends this message: "Happy Birthday. I was with you."'

At that my husband smiled and said, 'It was my birthday and she always remembered.'

Gordon changed our lives that day He was able to pass on messages from Mum that allowed me to put aside my fears and, more importantly, get over my guilt. She proved the point to my husband, as she said she would, that death is not final. I truly believe Mum guided us to that seminar, knowing I would be ready to accept her message with my husband at my side protecting me, and that he would not be able to argue or explain away what he heard that night.

I thank Gordon for acting as the catalyst that made all this possible, but most of all I thank Mum for being just as strong and determined in death as she was in life. She will live in our hearts forever.

As an aside to this I must say that I talk to Mum every day now and often feel her presence. This would have freaked me out in the past, but since hearing Gordon explain it all and reading his books I have been OK with it.

I have also seen Gordon since, in the hope that Mum would send another message, but also now understand she doesn't have to send messages all the time because she is always there. At the time of my first message the need was great. She needed to tell me she was OK and did not blame me and I needed to hear this from her. Thank you, Gordon, thank you...

It is always a joy when a message changes someone's life in such a profound way. And it was in Cape Town on my previous visit that I passed on a message that also had life-changing impact. It all took place one fine evening in a beautiful place called Seapoint. In the audience was Jess Morgan, and she was one scared lady. I'll let her tell the story:

In December 2003 an amazing and trouble-free pregnancy turned into a nightmare when terrible upper-abdominal pain led to a seizure. At 32 weeks, unbeknown to me, my son was removed by emergency Caesarean, and I didn't see him for four days when they let me out of ICU for a brief visit to the Neonatal Intensive Care Unit. He was minute, but a real fighter. Nature had developed his lungs early and we were able to take him home after three weeks.

Thirteen months later I was pregnant again and, given the rapid and unpredictable deterioration of my first pregnancy, my gynaecologist wanted a second opinion from a leading haematologist. He recommended terminating the pregnancy as it was very high risk and we would most likely 'lose the foetus by the seventh month anyway'.

Faced with a terribly difficult and daunting time ahead, my husband and I withdrew from everyone and did not celebrate the second pregnancy as we had the first. Then, in 2005, during this quiet and scary time, there were a number of synchronicities that resulted in a friend treating me to an evening in Seapoint with Gordon Smith.

As the session was drawing to a close, Gordon began a reading for me by saying: 'You have just started taking four different types of medication. I'm confused. I can see the pills lined up – but there's nothing wrong with you!'

Next he said, 'There's a baby coming.' There was much more to the reading – lots of validation, all amazing – but what I walked away with were two statements resounding in my ears: 'There's nothing wrong with you,' and 'There's a baby coming.'

It was an extremely unpleasant pregnancy, with four different types of pills to take in the morning (just as Gordon had foreseen) and a daily injection in my lower abdomen. I felt physically ill all the time, but I just kept saying to myself, like a mantra, 'There's nothing wrong with you and there's a baby coming!'

Just a month short of the due date my baby was removed by Caesarean as a precautionary measure. I was awake during the procedure and was able to witness the incredible moment of a new life entering our world. He weighed in at 2.9 kg, more than double my first son's weight, and, a year later is a strong, healthy, gentle, beautiful soul.

Gordon, thank you for the peace of mind and, therefore, our beautiful gift.

I have a photograph of that baby on my computer. He's a one-year-old with bright blue eyes and the biggest grin you could imagine under his white baseball cap, and his name is Seb. I keep that picture on my screen to remind me that the gift bestowed on me is not just about talking to the dead but helping the living.

*****

Talking about Seb reminds me of a life-changing message that I once gave in San Francisco.

The first time I gave a demonstration of mediumship in San Francisco, it was to a crowded room of about 1,000 people. It is very hard to distinguish people's faces in such a crowd and so when I returned a year later and was confronted by a woman and her partner thanking me for helping her to get pregnant, I had no idea what they were going on about!

Like most working mediums I have no recollection of most of the information that has been passed through me. On occasion a certain person or message will stay in my mind for a short while and I might find that message or situation useful in helping others who have encountered similar problems in their life. But generally a medium passes information to the recipient and then moves on to the next message.

In San Francisco the couple greeted me at the end of my demonstration and introduced themselves as Karen and Don. They said that they had seen me the previous year and that their life had changed so much since our last meeting. While I didn't want to take anything away from their obvious enthusiasm, I had to explain that I really couldn't remember the message they had received. This didn't seem to matter to Karen, who pushed out her swollen belly and said, 'Look!' I must say it was hard to miss it. She must have been at least six months pregnant. And I didn't even have to be psychic to notice this.

She couldn't wait to tell me that in her message the previous year her mother had come through from the spirit world and told her that she had an appointment for a fertility clinic two weeks later, but that she wouldn't have to go through with the treatment.

Her mother had died less than a year before and Karen had been desperate for some contact with her as she had been left so depressed by the loss, and also she had had three failed pregnancies during her mother's long illness and wanted to know if her mother could somehow help her to conceive from the other side.

Don told me that he was at his wit's end at the time and that his partner had become obsessed with becoming pregnant and also with seeking psychic help in the hope of reaching her beloved mother. He looked like a very patient man and he obviously loved Karen and was willing to help her any way he could. That's why when he had seen an advert on the Internet saying that I was going to be in their home town he had purchased tickets at once.

At that point Karen burst in again and took up the story. She said she had known it was her mother coming through as soon as she had heard me asking if there was anyone in the audience who knew a woman in the spirit world by the name of Nancy, who was trying to get in touch with her daughter who had just had a birthday that week.

It turned out that Karen's birthday had been the day before the demonstration and her mother's name was indeed Nancy. Through me, she went on to explain how she had died and gave details of the family she had met on the other side, all of which Karen accepted. What she couldn't understand at the time, though, was her mother's message that she wouldn't have to go through with the fertility treatment. This was hard for her to accept, she told me, as she was looking at it in a negative way. Her fear was that the clinic would tell her that she was not going to be able to carry a child full-term and that she and Don would have to go down the long road of adoption. This was something she really didn't want to consider, as she had been feeling exhausted after all the failed pregnancies, and then the loss of her mother to cancer had taken its toll on her and the rest of the family.

The actual message, she said, was that she had this appointment and that she wouldn't have to have any treatment. Her mother also said that she would be getting some very good news in two months' time – news that would change her life forever and help her to move forward. Thinking that she had no chance of conceiving a child without the help and expense of fertility treatment, Karen assumed that the news was to do with the adoption angle.

Then, when she visited the clinic a fortnight later, a treatment plan was offered to her, and so she dismissed my message completely. It had been great to hear from her mother, but the fact that she was now being accepted for the treatment made her doubt the message.

In the six weeks that followed that first visit to the clinic, Karen and Don were asked to make certain changes in their lives that might help them physically and emotionally before the treatment began.

But eight weeks after she had received her message from the other side, Karen began to feel different and to suspect that she was pregnant. A visit to her doctor confirmed that she had indeed become pregnant before her fertility treatment had begun.

Nancy's message that Karen would be given news in two months' time that would change her life forever was now coming true and, more than that, she now knew exactly what her mother had meant by not having to go through with the treatment. For the couple it was a double whammy! Not only had they made contact with Nancy in the spirit world, but she had been able to tell them that their long-held dream of starting a family was going to happen, and in a natural way.

By the time Karen and Don came back to see me, she had gone through all of the dangerous stages where she had miscarried in the past, and mother and baby were doing well.

Karen now believed that she and her mother were connected again and were undertaking the pregnancy together. As she said, 'To know that my mother is watching over me and my baby growing inside me has made me strong – strong enough to bring this new life into the world.'

*****

Most people are overjoyed when a loved one comes through at an event, but sometimes people are too inhibited or taken aback to respond, and they fail to make themselves known. I can usually tell when this is happening, but if a person won't come forward there's nothing I or the spirit world can do.

Wendy Whittle, a South African watercolour artist, was one such person – at first anyway. She saw me when I appeared on South African TV in 2004, on SABC3's *Three Talk with Noleen*. Wendy had never thought much about mediums and psychics. Even though she had been brought up in a metaphysical home and attended a metaphysical Sunday school and church, she had shied away from communicating with spirits. But that day in 2004, something compelled her to watch Noleen's show.

When the programme ended Wendy says she couldn't get what I had been saying out of her head and some unknown force propelled her to reserve a seat at my event that weekend. As she took her seat in the auditorium she wondered what on earth she was doing there. She was still a sceptic and her family was both bemused and amused by her attendance. But something was telling her she had to be present.

After the break, well into the second half of the reading, I received a message from a woman who had passed over with a blockage in her throat. She had been unable to say goodbye to her family and that had distressed her greatly. Now she desperately wanted them to know she was fine and whole and able to communicate with ease again.

In the audience Wendy heard the message and her heart leaped and pounded. She knew it was her mother coming through. She had been on a respirator before passing and her throat had been blocked with an end-tracheal tube. She had tried so hard to talk to Wendy as she drifted in and out of consciousness, but had been unable to do so.

Yet instead of standing up, Wendy sat in silence. She just couldn't accept it. 'No. It's not a message for me,' she said to herself and crossed her arms firmly across her chest.

On stage I sensed this and called out, 'Is this message for the lady with the crossed arms?'

'No!' came the emphatic reply from Wendy. And so I had no choice but to move on to someone else.

Wendy left the auditorium with her mind in turmoil.

Her heart said, 'It was Mum!' and her head said, 'No, it wasn't!'

For months she hashed the incident over in her mind. Then one day she just knew without doubt that her mother was trying to get through to her and that she absolutely had to get her message.

I had left South Africa by then, but Wendy started studying the spirit world in every aspect, reading everything that she could on spiritual development. Her family didn't share her interest and enthusiasm, though, and although Wendy's heart said, 'This is right and true,' her head still niggled, 'Why doesn't anybody else in the family believe what I believe? Maybe they're right after all. Maybe I'm just imagining I'm on the right path.' At times she became despondent. The spiritual path seemed a very lonely one and doubts began to creep in.

Then, in 2006, to her absolute delight she read in *Odyssey* magazine that I was once again visiting South Africa. She made sure she was amongst the first to book seats at the Sandton Convention Centre for 18 August. Before the event she prayed deeply that confirmation would come through to her that she was on the right path with her spiritual development. Who better, she reasoned, to confirm this than the spirit world itself?

On the night Wendy and a cousin of hers sat spellbound though the first half of the demonstration, but didn't receive any readings. Nevertheless Wendy wasn't worried. The first half of the evening seemed to be reserved for those who had lost loved ones recently, tragically and suddenly and who very much needed comfort right then and there. Wendy just knew that something would happen for her in the second half.

And she wasn't disappointed. Soon after the break she began to feel light touches over her forehead and cheeks, a little like spider webs, and then the atmosphere about her became very dense and very hot. She began to perspire and had to fan herself.

On stage I said, 'Mrs Jones – a Mrs Jones is calling her name.' Wendy knew straight away it was her maternal grandmother. She takes up the story:

The reading that followed was absolutely wonderful. Granny was always called 'Mrs Jones' by everyone, not by her first name, which she reserved only for very close family and friends. So she would have expected a young man like Gordon to address her as 'Mrs Jones'! She mentioned family and friends by name and there was absolutely no mistaking it was her. Gordon saw her as the matriarchal figure of a very large family, and this is the way that I, and the rest of the family, remember her.

She mentioned my husband, David, by name and gave me an accurate and a little amusing message pertaining to him. She spoke of being with me when I bought a crystal in a shop recently – something I had lovingly done a few weeks before. She mentioned my watercolour paintings and promised to help me with these, so that I could produce something really special. I had had a block with ideas for illustrating the book I am working on, but now new ideas are coming into my mind all the time and I know that when I sit in my studio again my brushes are being guided!

She also mentioned our family in Canada and then spoke of her psychic abilities. She was Welsh in this life and a metaphysician. And now – so importantly – she told me that I was on the right path with my studies. This was a direct answer to the question I had asked in my prayers before attending the event – word for word! She said I had inherited her psychic ability and that the veil between the worlds was getting thinner, which I believe it is. This was confirmation at its very best. When my grandmother's energy was withdrawn and Gordon moved on to the next reading, I wept tears of gratitude, joy and relief. I now feel so confident that I am progressing in the right direction, in spite of what anyone who does not believe says. My spiritual understanding is growing in leaps and bounds every day.

Words are inadequate to thank Gordon for this message that he passed on to me from the spirit world.

That message got through loud and clear and the recipient was waiting for it. But it doesn't always work that way. One extraordinary thing that happened during my African stay occurred during a live television appearance. I had been persuaded to do some live readings on a show when I got a weird sensation and heard myself saying to the host, 'You're going to lose your cameras in a second.' I was getting it from a boy who was walking around in the spirit world and demanding attention. He was looking for his brother and at the same time demanding to speak to his mum and dad.

Anyway, sure enough, at that point the power went down. Out went the cameras and the lights. While they got it all working again I said to the spirit, 'OK, son, I'll do what I can. Just give me the names.' He gave me names and they got his parents on the phone – this is live TV, remember. Actually his mother phoned in and said, 'That's my son you're talking about.' So with the boy's parents on speakerphone at their home, I had the boy through and it turned out to be, if I remember correctly, the first anniversary of his passing. He gave them lots of information and naturally they were astonished. But what surprised me was how he had been able to grab people's attention by making the power go down for a short while.

*****

My visit to South Africa was not, however, all about passing on messages at public demonstrations. I had gone there to help raise funds for a good cause – the Noah Foundation, a charity which provides for children who have been made orphans by AIDS and who often have the disease themselves. It's a heart-wrenching job because you are surrounded by deprivation and as one person you simply don't have the means to make them well, although your initial reaction is that you need to do something. They brought me one gorgeous little three-year-old boy who had been found a couple of days earlier cuddling the body of his mother who had died of AIDS.

The experience proved to be one for which I have lasting reason to be grateful. By our standards those children had nothing – there weren't even any beds: the children were sleeping on a concrete floor until Hay House bought them some mats. But I have to say that my initial reaction of horror at their circumstances was wrong: I soon discovered that although there was precious little I could do for them, they were able to do a lot for me. They taught me a great lesson. It's all too easy to be self-defeating when faced with conditions like that, even to start crying. That is not only a waste of energy, it's a waste of the valuable education such an experience affords.

What struck me more than anything else was that those children had such amazing spirit. Even though most of them didn't have long to live and – again by our standards – none of them had much to live for, they were happy, smiling, bubbling little people and it forced me to reflect on how selfish the rest of us can be.

I thought I had gone there for them, but their message was for *me*. There was absolutely nothing I could do to cure them or even to take away their suffering, but that wasn't the answer to the problem that confronted me. Looking at it as a medium, I could see that they were well prepared for the next part of their lives, which would not be in this world. They were taught in groups about HIV, AIDS and death and they absorbed it just as normal schoolchildren absorb their ABC. And then they got on with what they had, singing, laughing and dancing as they did so.

When we watch fund-raising programmes such as *Comic Relief* and *Children in Need* – all very worthy, don't get me wrong – we are shown clips which make us sad. They're meant to, so we will dig deep into our pockets. But when you go to South Africa and see kids with AIDS, you can't help but be moved by their spirit. They have overcome what weighs us down – the 'burden' of death, which will come to all of us. These kids are a clear illustration that there is life after death. Death can't really touch them. They've lost everything – their parents, families, friends, homes – and yet they are the finest example of the human spirit at its best. They didn't need messages from me, they didn't need convincing that death is not the end.

I was thinking about that during a demonstration in America when I was confronted by a woman who obviously came from a privileged background. She was probably in her late twenties, quite pretty, with long blonde hair and, on the surface, everything to live for, and yet all she had to express was woe. 'Why can't I be happy? Why does nobody love me? Why am I so lonely?'

I told her that the answer was clear: she didn't love herself. Why, I asked, was she giving up on herself?

'I'm not – everyone's giving up on me! My husband left me, I can't get a boyfriend, my sisters don't want to know me...'

As she rattled on, all I could think about was the happy faces of those unfortunate (unfortunate?) children in Africa singing their hearts out for me, a full-blown gospel choir singing *a cappella* with all the gusto they could muster.

Here was this woman who on the surface had everything but wanted more, more, more, and all the children in my mind wanted was to hold my hand. The theme of the seminar she had turned up to was 'I Can Do It' and I applauded her courage for having travelled some distance to attend it. And yet she came with such a negative attitude. She was just a huge gaping hole sucking in everything she could get but giving nothing.

My experience with the children in Africa is a lesson I will cherish for the rest of my life. It certainly made me appreciate what I have in my life. It also helped me to see how important this life is – no matter who you are or what your circumstances are. I would have to say it has been one of my most 'life-changing' messages to date.

As time goes by I hope to be able to pass on to people like that young lady the benefit of the rich experience my life has given me, to help people understand that we are here to learn, to expand, before we move on. The children of Noah moved me so much that I want to dedicate time and energy in helping them and bringing their plight to the attention of as many people as I can.

Even when you are dying, life can be lived with spirit.

CHAPTER 9

Finding those in need

THERE are some really special ladies in my life and one of them is Kate Terry, a smashing woman who helps me put together my weekly column for *Best* magazine. It is Kate who goes through letters from people who want to see me and decides on the ones who are the most in need. To verify her initial choices she will spend up to two hours talking to them on the telephone to ensure that she brings only genuine cases of grief to me. She also shepherds them to the Kensington hotel suite where I hold my weekly one-to-ones. After reassuring them that she has relayed *nothing* of their stories to me, she brings them into the room, where the sittings are recorded – for the people's benefit as much as *Best*'s. And then she weeps as she transcribes the recordings at home later.

Now this is not a woman who knew anything about mediumship before she was given the job of working with me, and I like it that way. To have employed anyone who had long been exposed to the kind of work I do would have been to risk a blasé spirit of 'Oh, we've heard all that before' creeping into the job. What's more, Kate's absolute integrity ensures that mistakes are never made. A careless slip allowing me to know a single detail of what I am about to relay from the spirit world would invalidate what I do and make a mockery of the precious gift that has been bestowed upon me.

Had it not been for Kate, I would never have met Carol...

If ever anyone was in need of a life-changing message it was Carol from Maidenhead. After a painful six-month illness with throat cancer, her husband Shuja died in April 2002. Just 16 months later her elder daughter Rana was murdered by her ex-boyfriend, who stabbed her 16 times while she was on her mobile phone to the police, having already reported him to them for stalking her.

How much tragedy can one woman take in so short a space of time? What message could the spirits deliver that would bring comfort to one who had suffered so much?

Of course Kate knew the story, but as part of our strict code of conduct had imparted none of it to me when she delivered Carol to my door.

Without any delay I was able to tell her that her elder daughter was with us. I could see the girl rubbing the front of a horse's face and smiling the most beautiful smile. She gave off a powerful energy that must have been felt by many people during her time on this side.

'She is surrounded by animals,' I said. 'Her grandmother is with her, but there is a man telling the old lady to allow the girl to come through.' 'It's her turn, let her through,' he was saying softly. I could see now that they were father and daughter and over the course of the next few minutes they made it clear to me that they wanted Carol to know they were happy, safe and free of any troubles.

'Your husband is taking me back to last summer,' I told her. '"I was with you giving you as much help as I could," he says. There's a photo in the sitting room and he says of it: "Yes, I know you talk to me." But it's the kitchen where everything happens. "I lean against the wall and watch you," he says. He's in awe of your strength – if it had been the other way round he could not have coped.'

Carol explained to me that she had fretted ever since her husband's death that she had forced him to live those last few months, hoping that he would pull through. Now she was thrilled to hear from him that he had been there for her. And the previous summer's big event that he referred to would have been the wedding of their younger daughter, Gemma.

'I'm so pleased he was with me,' she said, 'and, yes, I do talk to his photograph. The kitchen is the hub of the house, where we used to congregate. I would have loved Shuja to have said more in the reading but, as he made known, it was Rana's turn.'

'Your daughter had a love of horses,' I told Carol. 'One in particular. She shows me a picture of herself as a child – she was a tomboy. "I had a good life," she says. She won't talk about the terrible event which caused her to pass. "What's the point?" she says. She wants you to look at her life, not her death.' This is a sentiment that I repeat time and time again when relaying messages from the other side.

All she would say of the stalking killer was that 'There were eyes on me.' She was aware of that and tried to do something about it, but things happen that we just can't fathom.

'She wasn't frightened,' I said. 'She wants you to know.'

I learned later from Carol that Rana was walking her horse, Toby, back to the stables when the awful crime – for which the ex-boyfriend was subsequently convicted – took place.

'I decided to keep Toby,' Carol said. 'He has been my salvation. I muck out his stable every morning and being with him makes me feel closer to Rana. I just hope she thinks I'm doing a reasonable job!' She gave a rueful grin.

'She's very proud of how you are coping and managing,' I was able to reassure her.

As a further piece of evidence Rana had handed over a soft toy.

'I have some of Rana's furniture in my house,' Carol responded. 'In the spare room, which I call Rana's, sits a soft giraffe toy that her best friend Emma bought for her.'

'I can see a field,' I told her. 'Your husband and daughter are standing there with a dog. They walk through that field with you. You're never alone.'

'I have good days and bad days,' Carol wrote to me afterwards. 'But knowing that both Shuja and Rana are around me has helped enormously. Thank you, Gordon, for that reassurance.'

*****

For some reason the majority of people who pluck up the courage to be put in touch with their loved ones are women. So I was mildly surprised when Kate brought a man into the room one day. He was clearly distraught, which in the case of men is usually a sign that they have lost a child. But it was not a child who came through but another man.

I told the man that we were receiving a visit from someone 'who says he was extremely close to you'. 'One thing I can say,' I began, 'is that the two of you – well, it's as though you were one person.'

He said nothing, but tears were welling up in his eyes.

'He says your birthday is very significant to him and he seems to be saying that the two of you were Gemini.'

Still no response.

At that point I had to be frank, for it was a frank message I was getting: 'He knows you can feel his pain, but he wants you to leave the grave. Stop going to the grave, you are keeping him in the ground. He says you go to the graveside every day.'

Now there was a response: 'It's true. Since he died

I've never left the graveside. I do go there every day. I'm obsessed.'

The spirit then gave me still more astonishing information: 'He said you shared a bicycle, you shared everything.' He even gave me a street name and a house number. 'His departure was recent and you still feel his presence, but he can't get through to you clearly because every day you take him back to the grave and bury him all over again. You must see him alive, as he was. But now he's telling me you have the same birthday. Can it be true that you were both born on the same day?'

'Yes,' he said, 'we were. He was my identical twin.'

In the outer room his wife was waiting. She told Kate her husband's obsessive grief had been causing her great distress. If he wouldn't take her word for it that he had to move on from the grave, I hope he took his beloved brother's. If anyone needed a life-changing message, he did.

*****

Midge Noding from Maidstone in Kent was another of the people that Kate brought to see me. When we met I saw a cheerful woman in the prime of life with a mop of reddish auburn hair, friendly eyes and a welcoming smile.

I would never have guessed to look at her that her life had been crossed by tragedy and that her carefree exterior concealed a heavy heart.

When I took Midge's hand I felt a young man coming through and I sensed that he had never got to live his life out. 'It was cut short,' I told Midge. 'He's close, and he just wants to hold you. He is there and you're aware of him, because things happen around the house. I just saw his smile – he laughed a lot. "It's the way I passed to the spirit world that caused just too much pain," he says.'

What I didn't know was that I was in touch with Midge's younger son, Steven. Midge and her husband, Jim, had been devastated when he was killed in a car accident in 1989. He was just 19.

Unaware of this, I went on to tell Midge: 'He's taking me to a bedroom. This is where he is. There are times when he watches you. He's guiding you. There's music playing around him and he's trying to put thoughts into your head. You have a spiritual connection. He's singing and he's taking me to the month of December – something about Christmas had a special meaning. A part of you knew you wouldn't have him for long. He's with his gran. I feel as though he hugs people. He knew how to love, he had a special quality.'

Afterwards Midge told me that I had got her son's personality spot-on. 'He was gentle and he smiled and laughed all the time. We shared the same taste in music and he'd play it loudly while I sang along. That's what all the singing's about. And as for December and Christmas, Jim and I haven't wanted to spend Christmas at home since Steven passed away. Last year we went to Egypt. About "a part of me knowing I wouldn't have him for long" – well, I used to dream about his funeral long before he died.'

But life had more tragedy for Midge and Jim. After Steven's death his elder brother, Anthony, was wracked with guilt. He felt he should have been killed and not Steven. He took up drugs and drink, and Midge and Jim grew to live in fear of a knock on the door bringing news that Anthony too had died. In July 2004 their worst nightmare came true when they learned that their elder boy was indeed dead. In the space of 15 years they had lost both their precious children.

I knew nothing of this when I told Midge that there were two men taking turns to come through. They were like chalk and cheese but felt like one. Then I realized that they were her sons and that one had died just two years previously.

'The son who died two years ago says, "I'm sorry, Mum." He never meant to hurt you. He knew what you'd gone through,' I told Midge. 'He struggled a bit, but he's free now and fine. His brother was waiting for him to take him over. He's sending thoughts to David and he's talking about a certificate that Steven has. I can hear him roaring with laughter. A handwritten card is important. "Tell Paul I was asking for him and mention the car," he says.

'He's showing me a hat. "Give her that, then she'll know it's me," he says. "Ask her about my T-shirt." He says it's his. I want to shave my hair off. There's a birthday in October and both your sons will be very much around you at this time.

'They're sending thoughts to Simon and Jackie, and Will or William. The son with the short hair hugs you and says, "I haven't gone." You could just open a door and imagine him there and he will be.

'They're taking me into a garden and handing me a long-stemmed rose. You're a special person to have got through what you have.'

Midge was gobsmacked: 'Where to start?! I do have a nephew called David. My brother Paul has just bought a new car. Simon is my nephew and Jackie is my friend.

They had an Uncle Bill, which must be William. Steven was very proud of his GCE certificates and they used to hang in his room. I've only found one card from Steven, yet he wrote loads. I have a few from Anthony. Steven wore a cap and Anthony had a shaved head.'

'And what about the T-shirt?' I reminded her.

'I was hoping he'd forget that! It's a disgusting old thing that Jim still wears around the house! My birthday is in October and I always go into the garden and chat with the boys. I've just got to thank you, Gordon. It's so comforting to know that they are together and with my mum, Clarrie. I just wish that they were here to give me those flowers themselves.'

*****

Like Midge, so many of the people Kate brings to me have had great tragedy to cope with in their lives. One of these was Maggie Levendoglu. I remember well the meeting I had with Maggie, an attractive woman in her forties who lived in Horley, the Surrey town that has become so much a suburb of Gatwick airport. She told me how her three-year-old granddaughter Lauren regularly talked to her father Dave, Maggie's son, who had died in a car crash.

Maggie had doted on Dave, whom she described as a 'wonderful boy'. He had had a good job at the airport and a great circle of friends, the best of whom was Richard. Dave had been engaged to a 'lovely girl', Kelly, and, of course, they had Lauren, whom Dave idolized, just as his mother idolized him. 'He was a great dad,' Maggie recalls.

When I met Maggie, Dave had been only a memory since a tragic night in February 2006 when the car driven by Richard crashed, killing them both. Dave was just 26.

Further tragedy was to follow. When the crash happened, Richard had just become a father again, but ten weeks later his baby daughter died of cot death.

Although her son was dead, Maggie felt sure that he was somehow still around. And what was more, three-year-old Lauren often spoke to her dad and told Maggie quite matter-of-factly that she often saw him. Little children are often so much more open-minded as regards these things.

Maggie had never been a writer or anything like that, but now, often as she was driving in the car, a poem would pop into her head and later she would write it down. Was Dave sending her poetry he had written? Maggie felt sure that he was.

Friends told her that things would get easier with time, but when I saw her Dave's memory was still fresh and raw in her mind. No matter how hard she tried to be happy that her son was in a better place, she found it hard to stop the tears flowing.

As usual, I knew nothing of Maggie's story when we met. But as soon as I took her hand I felt a young man come close to us. I got the name 'David' and that he was Maggie's boy, her son, and not yet at the first anniversary of his death. I told Maggie he didn't want to talk about how he died, but he wasn't ill, or suffering, and 'Granddad' had been there to meet him.

As soon as I said the name 'David', Maggie knew that her son was there. He had been known to everyone as 'Dave' – to everyone but her, that is. To her he had always been 'David'. And 'Granddad' was her father, who'd died in 2004. He and his grandson had had their differences when David was a teenager, but recently they'd become great friends and golfing buddies.

Maggie felt better already, but there was still more to come. 'David says he loves the photograph you've put up. It's special,' I told her. He talked about other photos too, one of him with long hair, which made him laugh, and one in uniform wearing a beret.

Maggie knew exactly what he was talking about. 'They're in an alcove!' she exclaimed. 'There's the school photograph, where he had longer hair. And the one in uniform is one when he was in the Boy's Brigade. He hated that beret!'

Now David was showing me a memorial plaque with a beautiful tribute and then a special tree that seemed to make him smile.

Maggie explained: 'He worked for BAA at Gatwick and they've put a memorial plaque up, and at the golf club where he and my dad used to play they've planted a tree in his memory!'

'Now,' I told Maggie, 'he says that one of the last cards he gave you has a special meaning. It's in the drawer.'

Maggie gasped. 'When he died, Kelly, that's his fiancée, went to empty his car and found two Valentine's cards, one for her and one for Lauren. It wasn't like him to be prepared – maybe he knew something. I've always kept the cards in a drawer.'

'Finally,' I said, 'there's somebody else with him in the spirit world – another young person. And another mother is crying. Your boy would never hurt anybody in the world and to see others cry makes him cry. He's really trying to help people.'

Maggie told me about Richard and his ten-week-old child. 'That's so like David,' she said. 'The fact he wants to reassure me that he's OK and wants to help people is just so him! You've captured his personality and sentiments so exactly.'

At last Maggie can stop mourning her son. He's happy, not suffering, and just wants her to be happy too. Now she feels that she can fulfil his wish. That's what mediumship is really about – reassuring those left behind that their loved ones are in a place of hope, peace and freedom from the suffering of this material world. It's a great feeling when you can bring an end to unnecessary grief. And often a simple message will suffice.

*****

Sometimes messages from the other side can be quite brief, but at other times there's so much detail it's quite overwhelming. Take Toni Stefano's dad, Ronnie. When he came through for his daughter the scene was like an unexpected meeting of two old friends who've been apart for ages – two people who have so much to catch up on that neither can get a word in edgeways.

Ronnie Stefano died suddenly in May 2005. He was

only 41. Toni, who lives in the Essex town of Dagenham, is 24, so she and Ronnie were close in age as well as affection. When he passed she was devastated and missed him badly. The worst of it was that his sudden death gave her no chance to say goodbye. To get any sort of message from him, however brief, seemed terribly important to her.

When I met Toni I didn't know any of this, of course, but as soon as I took her hand a boyish-looking man came forward. I sensed that he was in his forties, but he seemed younger than his years, partly because of his sunny nature. He was carrying a bangle and I felt it was special.

When I told Toni, she was immediately excited. 'It's my dad, definitely. He always wore bangles. I've still got them!'

Now Ronnie was saying that he needed to give his daughter the message that he wasn't suffering. He knew Toni wasn't sleeping properly and that she talked to him in the early hours. He wanted her to know that when she did that he was sitting there with her.

'He knows about the computer,' I told Toni. 'You've compiled something. I can hear music being played.'

'I've made a website of music as a tribute to Dad,' Toni explained. But before she could elaborate, Ronnie came back with even more news.

'He's being really daft,' I told his daughter. 'He's trying to bring an image back to your mind of him fooling around, not being dead. He sees a lovely snap of him holding you when you were a baby and a little photo of him on his own, a degree, an academic one, travelling, a passport being stamped, a tattoo, a guitar, two houses, two homes. I can see a funny Valentine card, L plates being thrown away and he's giving me names: Michael, Colin, David...'

'There's too much!' protested Toni. 'The photo of me as a baby is in his room and the little photo of him is in my purse. He used to strum the guitar for fun. The academic thing – I'm in the middle of my teacher's exam for dancing. My tattoo is recent – ballet shoes. I think the two homes are mine and his girlfriend's. He came to live with me when he was ill. The funny Valentine card was one he sent to my mum, Adele. He still had a great relationship with her. The L plates are my boyfriend Dave's. If Dad's showing them being chucked away, it looks as though Dave's going to pass his driving test next month, then! Travelling, passports – that's Cyprus. We're buying a house there. Michael, Colin and David: Michael's my dad's cousin and Colin and David are his brothers. What else?'

'Well,' I said, 'there's someone else who died young, close to the age your father was when he passed. And there's a grandfather in the spirit world who had terrible breathing problems. I can hear a song by Mariah Carey: "Shining down on you from heaven".'

'Dad lost a half-brother 15 years ago, and he was only 42, so that's the one who died young,' said Toni. 'But what I'm amazed about is you picking up on my granddad. He was a Ronnie, too, and he died from angina, which made him awfully breathless. And that Mariah Carey song always reminds me of him.'

'Your dad's got such a busy mind,' I told Toni. 'He says he tried to accomplish so many things in one day but he never managed it. He never finished things and now he's embarrassed at the mess he's left behind. He couldn't foresee everything.'

Toni looked thoughtful. 'He was such a clever man – he knew the answer to everything. You know what? I think that's him making a joke. It's so typical of him!'

Ronnie Stefano's great regret was that if he had not died so suddenly, young Toni would have been able to come to know him as a friend as well as a father. I hope that after our meeting that is exactly how she will be able to think of him.

CHAPTER 10

Trusting in spirit

COME with me on the magical journey to America I took last May. At first I stayed and worked at the Venetian Hotel in Las Vegas. More than 7,000 people attended the seminar addressed by a range of us from both sides of the Atlantic, including Louise Hay, the founder of Hay House, the publishing company that produced this book. Louise's most famous book, *You Can Heal Your Life*, has gone out to some 40 million people and changed so many lives. She is such a positive and incredible woman and a real inspiration to me.

It was just before this seminar that I flew out to Malibu and met Shirley MacLaine. But the main reason for my trip was to take part in this fantastic event, which Louise had entitled 'I Can Do It' – a very positive statement for those who came along to learn to believe in themselves. Many of the Hay House authors gave fascinating talks on life and inspired the audiences with their own brand of philosophy. Of course, I was asked to give workshops and demonstrations of mediumship, something I love to do in America, as I always find that the people there are so receptive to what I do.

While I was introducing myself to the audience during my first demonstration and explaining how mediumship worked, I got the strange feeling that someone was standing beside me. This sometimes happens when I work, particularly when spirits are incredibly anxious to get their message across. I stopped short and asked my guide if he wanted me to start the demonstration already.

I really hadn't even begun to tune in when I heard 'Josh' being called in my ear. I repeated the name out loud and then I heard the name 'Diane'. Again I repeated the name and in a flash a black lady in the middle of the crowd raised her hand.

I found I was speaking spontaneously. 'Your name is Diane and your son is Josh. He is here in a military uniform and you carry a photo of him dressed like that in your bag. He wants his brother to know he is fine and says that he must stop being angry and get on with his life. He has put everything on hold and Josh wants him to get back to what he was doing before his death.'

Diane was so relieved to hear this. She told me that Josh had died in Iraq eight months earlier whilst serving in the army. He had been just 22 years old. She had come to the seminar with just one hope: to get a message from him. She took a photo from her bag and showed it to me. It showed a very handsome soldier.

Diane said that when Josh had died, his brother had been so overcome with grief and eventually depression that he had given up his studies. That's why she had been desperate for Josh to come to her and let her know that he was aware of his brother's condition. She hoped that might encourage her younger son to turn his life around. Now she was full of hope. She had recorded the message on a small tape recorder she had brought with her and was planning to let her younger son hear it.

I don't know what the outcome of that was, but for me the special thing about this message was seeing a loving mother being connected to a son who had died in another country where she had no chance to say good-bye or hold him. This is where I feel that there is such value in mediumship. When someone is given one more chance to communicate with a loved one, something beautiful and healing takes place.

*****

During my second demonstration I encountered – as sometimes happens – a man who had not been struck by recent grief but who was dreadfully afraid of dying, paralysed by the fear of it. He termed it 'external extinction'. Fortunately, I was able to give him a number of messages that turned him around in minutes. The certain knowledge that people he knew who had died were able to communicate with him and provide proof not only of their identity but also of the fact that they still very much existed took away the fear that he had had for so long.

Someone told me afterwards that he had actually been in therapy for years in a bid to overcome his terror, all to no avail. Psychiatrists are patient people who wait for the people they are treating to sort things out in their heads. I can cut to the chase – I have to in a window of time that is rarely more than half an hour. When the spirit world tells me what is troubling a loved one and I pass it on without mincing my words, they rarely deny it. And once the problem has been identified, it can be solved.

Two brothers who came to see me once went away

with a very different message from the one they had expected. They had lost their mother a year previously and were stuck in grief. They could not get her out of their minds and they dearly wanted to know if she had crossed safely to the other side and was happy.

The lady came through and did reassure them about her own wellbeing, but she also delivered what I can best describe as a 'loving lecture'. They had a sister called Sally, she told me, and she had a teenage daughter who had a serious illness. The pair confirmed that this was indeed the case and that they were extremely concerned about the welfare of their niece – indeed, one of them wept openly and told me he had been unable to sleep for worrying about the girl, because her mother was refusing to address the problem.

The lady who came through was adamant. She said the illness could be cured, but it would go on getting worse if the mother – her daughter, of course – failed to get medical treatment for the problem.

What I saw here was that the girl's mother, who had refused to come and see me with her brothers, was using her daughter's illness to get extra attention for her grief. This does happen more often than I would care to mention. She was grieving for their mother, but she was able to get more attention by saying, 'And look how sick my daughter is.'

The lesson to be learned here is that grief can bring out the worst in us if it is not dealt with. I could do nothing more than send loving thoughts to Sally and her sick daughter, but I hope her brothers were able to convince her that since all was well with their mother the grieving could stop, for that seemed to present the only chance of her daughter getting well.

*****

The messages I get are not always for the grieving – they can, on occasions, be very practical. My late friend, the absolutely brilliant medium Albert Best, has always been very helpful when it comes to things that have been lost. During the US tour a woman told me she had been asked to keep several thousand dollars which belonged to her daughter and she was at her wits' end because she couldn't find the money. She'd put it somewhere safe, she said, but she just couldn't remember where, and she was in all kinds of trouble because her daughter said she needed it.

I got nothing through, so I tuned in to Albert and

said, 'Please help me here, you're good at this sort of thing.'

What I got back was, 'Tell the lady her son-in-law has already been to the house and taken that money.'

So I told her, 'You've not lost the money and you're not losing your mind. Your son-in-law has collected it.'

The woman contacted me days later to say that had indeed been the case and that she was greatly relieved. Her life had been in great danger of being changed if she hadn't got that message, so thank you, Albert.

*****

This never happened to Albert, but some very good mediums have, for one reason or another, lost faith in their own abilities. I remember an Irish medium – she was one of the best I had ever come across and very honourable – telling me she had once been 100 per cent certain of the message she had been giving to a woman, but the woman had denied everything, saying, 'That's so untrue. You're a fraud, you're a phoney.'

The medium had just crumbled. She hadn't been able to believe she had been let down by the spirits, so she had taken some time off and examined what she was doing, and said to herself, 'If that woman was so adamant that what I was getting was wrong and could harm her, then I'm not going to do it again,' and had packed it all in.

Three years later she had wondered about starting again and said to the spirit world, 'Give me a sign to let me know if this is the right thing to do.'

After that she had met the woman 'by chance' in a supermarket. The woman had come up to her and said, 'I've been trying to contact you, but I've lost your number. What I wanted to say to you was that every single thing you told me was right, I just didn't know it.'

The whole message had tied up in quite an amazing way and the woman concerned had been feeling really guilty for not accepting it, especially when she had learned that in the three intervening years the medium had never given another message.

As a result of that encounter the medium had gone back to doing what she had always done so well, but, she told me, she had had to ask herself how strong her faith had been, given that she had so easily lost her belief.

I've also given messages to people who've said, 'No, I don't have a clue what you're talking about,' but long ago I reached the point where I established great trust in what comes through and I also realized that what I say to people rarely has anything to do with me. It's coming *through* me, not *from* me and therefore it's their responsibility to go and establish the truth of it. A lot of people want you to say things that they can immediately identify with, but it's part of their responsibility to go and check on the information I have given them.

Still, when that medium told me that story, it was a good lesson for me. I had asked her if she had been off the circuit for three years because she had been ill, and she had said, 'Kind of, I just felt depressed, let down.' But what had happened was that she had let herself down by losing her faith. The flip side of that, though, is that later she reconnected to her strength in a much better way than she could ever have anticipated.

What people often don't realize is that the greatest part of a medium's development is their own life. That woman had to go off and live her life for a while, just go off into the wilderness to discover how strong her faith really was. In spite of the fact that she had already been a good medium for some time, she was made to do some self-examination. And her life experience in those three years actually stood her in great stead later on. It defeated every bit of doubt she had been entertaining without realizing it. I know, I've been there, but thankfully I've always been able to conquer it. From time to time, however, I need to disconnect from spirit and recharge my batteries, to remind myself that I am alive and living in the physical world.

And that's how I felt when I came home from my American sojourn.

CHAPTER 11

Dreams, nightmares and fears

SPIRIT often delivers messages to us through dreams. A girl came to me on one occasion and said, 'Gordon, last night I dreamed of my father, but it was the strangest dream. He was wearing designer sunglasses and leathers and riding a Harley-Davidson motorbike and laughing his head off. It was strange because my father, who died quite recently, was blind.'

Now I didn't have to summon up too much expertise to work this dream out. On questioning, the girl told me that her father had often said during his life that if he wasn't blind he would like to ride a Harley from one side of America to the other. His spirit had come through to tell her that he was happy and totally free of the disability he had suffered on Earth.

On another occasion two women came to see me, a

mother and her daughter. The mother's husband – the younger one's father – had come through with lots of information which made them happy, but I sensed that the daughter was still troubled. When I asked her what it was, she told me that she was having a recurring dream in which she was a salmon trying to swim upstream with many others, but each time she tried to leap up to the next level her mother, who was standing by the bank, held out a net to prevent her from reaching it.

'How long have you been having this dream?' I asked.

'On and off for the three years since my father died,' she replied.

That was another easy one to work out. Although her mother assured me that she loved her daughter and would never do anything to hold her back, she was doing precisely that. She was clinging to her daughter as she had once clung on to her husband, and it was his spirit that was trying to show the girl that in the only way he could reach her – in her dreams.

*****

When people ask me if it is possible for our loved ones in the spirit world to contact us in our dreams, what I tell them is to remember how they felt during the dream rather than what they saw.

Going by what I have heard, the dreams that convince us that we have indeed had a visit from someone on the other side are those that leave us with a distinct emotion that stays with us longer than the dream itself. This is what prompts us to realize that something strange has occurred. It's that *otherly* sense that our rational mind fails to fathom or work out with the usual logic.

This type of feeling is one that I myself associate with the spirit world. Often when I tune in before a reading or public demonstration, I get a strong sense of something strange, a feeling that tells me that I am now linked to the other side. It is difficult to describe this feeling, as it is not connected to any human emotion that I recognize in my everyday life.

Eileen Walsh struggled to describe her feelings to me during a private sitting after I told her that her father in the spirit world was confirming that he had visited her in a dream. He showed me a picture of himself lifting Eileen out of a wheelchair and teaching her to walk. All of this looked as though it had occurred in a dream, I told her. As I said it, Eileen's jaw dropped and she cut in on my words, excitedly saying that this was exactly what *had* happened to her in a dream. Everything else I said during that sitting seemed to go by the wayside. Now all my sitter wanted to do was describe her dream to me.

Almost two years earlier Eileen had been involved in a horse-riding accident that had left her almost paralysed. Her left leg wouldn't work due to damage she had sustained to her lower back. For six months she was confined to a wheelchair and things were not looking good for her. Even though she had paid for the best medical attention money could buy and had begun to work with a physiotherapist whom she had brought to live with her, her spirit was dampened to such a degree that she just wanted to give up.

Almost a year after her accident she wasn't showing any sign of improvement and she found herself crying herself to sleep, thinking her life was over. She told me that she asked her father, who had died some ten years earlier, if he would come and take her to where he was. She said it was the first time she had thought of her dead father since her unfortunate accident and that she just wanted to die and be with him.

During the night, she woke several times and each time felt worse than the last when she thought that she would have to go through yet another day like the last, constantly wishing for her old life before the accident. In the very early hours of the morning she drifted into a kind of sleep where she could see herself sitting in her wheelchair in the middle of a field. She said that the field was like none she had ever been in before because it was so bright and the grass was a green so brilliant that she became transfixed by it. She felt a joy inside which she found hard to describe and then out of nowhere her father appeared, smiling at her with open arms and asking her to come to him.

She woke out of the dream with a start, tears running down her cheeks and an indescribable feeling in her gut. She wondered if she had almost died, given that she had asked her father to come for her and he had. She assumed that she had called him and that his appearance meant that she was to go to him.

More than the dream, it was the feeling inside her that stayed with her for the rest of the day – a feeling that she had never had before and could not compare with any other in her life.

Nothing much changed in her physical state for the next few weeks and then out of the blue one night the exact same dream occurred, leaving her with the same feeling when she woke. The only difference with this dream was that Eileen got up from the chair and stood for a moment on her own.

The day following the dream she found that for the first time in her therapy she wanted to stand; in fact, she stood for many minutes before she became tired and had to sit down again. She said that the feeling that had remained with her after the dream had been the force driving her on.

For the next few weeks she experienced the same dream over and over, only now her father encouraged her to walk, and each day that followed the dream she became stronger and began to walk further and further on her own. Each day that followed the dream was also accompanied by the same feeling in her gut that had followed her from the dream into real life.

I was fascinated listening to this story, especially when Eileen told me that when she no longer needed her wheelchair, the dream had ended and never come back to her. That, she said, was why she had to come and see me. She needed to know if I could tell her whether her father in the spirit world was actually involved, or if it was all in her imagination. Now I totally understood why she had behaved as she did when I had mentioned her father and the vision he showed me.

Even as I think of Eileen's story I wonder what the sceptics would say. Many would no doubt say that her subconscious mind had created the dream out of her frustration and desperation. Some might argue that she had just deluded herself into thinking that her dead father was giving her strength and that her condition could have been psychological and overcome by this trick of the mind.

I had never met Eileen before the sitting, nor knew that she had been in a wheelchair for a year of her life. I had no idea that her father was in the spirit world and I could never have imagined that she had had experiences with him in dream states that she believed had healed her. But, more than any of this, the thing that convinced me that something spiritual had happened was the indescribable feelings she experienced during her dreams. This truly made me believe that Eileen's father was helping her.

It really doesn't matter in cases like this what people believe, as long as they get better – and Eileen did. She believed that her father was helping her from the other side. I confirmed that as a medium and her life changed for the better.

*****

As well as bringing spirit communication, some dreams are prophetic. We do get moments of precognition when our bodies are sleeping. People talk about seeing the Twin Towers fall in New York before 9/11 and that doesn't surprise me. 'That wasn't due to a spirit,' I tell them. 'It was down to you, your own anxiety.'

How could people be anxious about an event that hadn't happened? Time is not relevant to consciousness. Spiritually only a fragment of us exists in time, in the human body. The parts of us that don't exist in time have knowledge of everything – past, present and future.

As for nightmares, they are based on the fear you take to bed with you. They come from a part of your psyche that is calling for attention – particularly when the nightmare is recurring. If you have a dream that you are falling off a cliff, for example, then you have a fear that you are falling in life, failing in life, if you like. If you dream of someone stabbing you to death, then you need to look at who it is your subconscious knows is trying to harm you. The man with the knife may be trying to kill your business, destroy your family, obliterate your love. And take into account that you yourself could be that man.

To give another example, perhaps you are holding a baby that someone is trying to harm. Your children may be grown up, but your subconscious wants you to be aware that someone is acting against their interests. Again, it could be themselves.

I went through a stage of having the recurring nightmare that somebody was trying to stab me in the back. I could never recognize the person because he was flamboyantly dressed and his face was concealed, but each time I turned my back he would plunge a knife into my back. I knew it was someone I knew, someone I liked, and I eventually worked out who it was and avoided them thereafter.

In another dream a dog was protecting me from a snake. The snake actually appeared to be very nice, so I would go to stroke it, but every time I did, it would bare its fangs and the dog would leap forward and pounce on it. The funny thing was that although the dog would get bitten and collapse on the ground, it would recover and the snake would disappear into the grass. The snake turned out to be a man who worked with me at the hairdresser's, someone who appeared to be a good friend but, I subsequently learned, was trying to sell scurrilous stories about me to a Sunday newspaper.

The dog was a symbol of the friends who were trying to protect me.

These are the sort of things that often cause nightmares – but don't forget you could also have them just because you were watching something frightening on television before you went to bed!

*****

Anger comes through a lot in dreams and it's an emotion I deal with quite often, because people who are grieving are usually angry underneath. 'Why did they die before I got there?' 'Why did God have to take them?' 'Why didn't the doctors save them?' But this is all anger that will dissipate in time. The anger that troubles me is the cold, buried anger that is not immediately evident, although I can usually spot it, because it is often revealed in controlled, measured voices. That's the dangerous stuff we have to be careful of.

Both kinds of anger actually have their roots in fear. Say you step off a pavement and a car comes along at speed and almost knocks you over. You are afraid of losing life and limb, and furious at the driver for not slowing down, but it passes. Deep-rooted rage doesn't. It can be there for life. Normally, we conduct our lives through a full deck of emotions, so imagine being stuck on one card – the anger card. Such people suffer greatly.

I remember the man who came to see me after his wife had hanged herself. I gave him a very nice message from her, but he was furious. Boiling over with rage, he swore at me and said, 'How dare you speak to my wife when I can't?' His eyes were popping out of his head as he called me every name under the sun. With a little help from Albert Best, I realized that this man was hellbent on trying to hurt the very person trying to help him, because he didn't wish to be free from his pain. He didn't want to let go.

Fortunately the story has a happy ending. Some time later he wrote me a nice letter of apology and said he now understood what had been going on inside himself. I was glad for him and for his wife, because she was now free to get on with her development in the afterlife.

That message changed both his life and hers.

CHAPTER 12

Words of proof

THAT old adversary of the psychic medium (any psychic medium), Chris French, popped up yet again on ITV's *This Morning* programme back in May, challenging me yet again to 'prove it'. Chris and I get on very well and I believe that we have a healthy respect for one another. Although I don't always take up such challenges, I know and trust that Chris would not try to trick me and he would make sure that we both had a good chance to represent our work. So I agreed to do it.

This time Chris decided to pretend to be a psychic medium himself. The producers had brought two ladies to the studio, Angela and Anna, and told them that we were both mediums who would give them a reading. They had been blindfolded in case either of them recognized Chris from his previous appearances.

Chris (who was using the name Derek O'Connor because he thought the 'con' bit appropriate to what he was about to do!) told Anna that he was being 'told' of a kitchen malfunction, that the name 'John' was cropping up (who doesn't know a John?), and that she was quite ambitious and had been 'bubbly' at a party (which was pretty obvious from her fun-filled face). He also talked of an 'unfinished book', which meant nothing to her, but he had struck lucky with the kitchen malfunction, because she'd had a washing machine break down in the recent past.

I sensed that this lady had no need of the grief counselling on which my work is focused, but I told her that I had the name 'Kennedy' coming through. That turned out to be her married name and I also gave her various other facts and figures that proved to be accurate.

As for Angela, I will skip over the misinformation Chris offered to her, but she was in genuine need of the message I gave her. It was principally about a man who had passed with a heart condition, a man with smiling eyes who used to sing the Helen Reddy song 'Angie, Baby' to her. Clearly demonstrating that they cannot be conned, the spirits who sent me that message reduced Angela to tears. Her father had died just six months earlier of heart failure and he was indeed a man with smiling eyes who used to sing 'Angie, Baby' to her.

To be fair, Chris put his hands up and admitted that his experiment hadn't gone as well as he'd hoped. He acknowledged that I had produced better evidence, whereas the trick stuff he had dished out was nothing more than cold reading. What's more, we agreed on a warning to anyone seeking the help of a medium to beware those who charge inordinate fees for putting a grieving one in touch with a loved one.

Incidentally, *This Morning*'s psychic experiment proved yet again that British television is still living in the dark ages as far as mediumship is concerned. Thanks to a decision dating back to the Lord Reith era of several decades ago, showing people like me at work is banned. Exorcisms can be shown (often being conducted by people who are mentally ill), as can human autopsies and even murder, but not a medium bringing through a message from a spirit to help someone who is grieving. Thus the ITV producers had to edit out the all-important bit when I gave Angela the message from her father. I also have to sign a disclaimer before I go on television giving the programme makers the assurance, in the case of a live appearance, that I will not communicate with anyone on the other side while I am on air. Why it is all so heinous that it cannot be shown on TV is beyond me. I hope that one day things will change.

*****

People seem to love to challenge psychics. Very recently I got a call from a leading European television presenter asking me if I would go to Paris and take part in what he described as a 'psychic challenge'. The idea, he said, was that I would face one or more people who would challenge me to do certain things. If I 'pulled it off' I would win 200,000 euros 'prize money'.

Now, I just don't do stunt shows for television. Having been subjected to the most rigorous tests over a period of more than five years by Professor Archie Roy and Trish Robertson, as I mentioned earlier, I feel confident in my gift and don't have any need to prove it.

Having said that, there is a certain satisfaction in being able to surprise the doubting Thomases. I was doing a television show some time back with a Scottish presenter. To be honest, it was not something I wanted to do, because it turned out to be one of those Halloween shows where they come up with all the daft spooky things such shows are renowned for. Anyway, at one point we were discussing mediumship and the presenter made a derogatory remark about it which annoyed me. It was, after all, the end of a very long and tedious day. Then he added that he didn't really believe in what I did.

At that point – bang! – I got a message through for him. It was his grandfather, who wanted him to know that within a week he would be sitting by a hospital bed in Connecticut. 'You know this person's ill and you're very frightened at the moment,' the message continued. It turned out to be his father and it was so spot-on that it reduced one of Scotland's top presenters to tears, although I was able to assure him that his dad was going to be fine, despite having heart problems.

The crew actually filmed all this, but the presenter snatched the tape, although he did talk about it to a newspaper later, saying it was 'amazing' and that I actually 'shook him up'.

*****

Messages can often shake people up, and mediums and others do have a certain responsibility in terms of what they pass on. This was really brought home to me back at the end of 2005, when a Mr Davies came to see me at a Spiritualist church in London six months after the death of his mother.

He hadn't told me that he had lost his mother, but she came through very quickly. I asked her to give me evidence of her life so that I could convince her son that it was truly her, but she wasted no time talking about how she died or giving other details, just insisted that I tell her son that she had been going to die anyway. She kept saying it over and over again until I relayed the message to him.

I remember thinking that this was very strange, but Mrs Davies wasn't worried about that. She went on to tell her son that what he had been told before was a load of rubbish and that he wasn't to take any notice of it. By now I must admit that I was becoming curious, to say the least. I wanted to know the story behind this private message. This is something I very rarely concern myself with. As I always tell people, it is not important for the medium to know what is going on. What is important is to get the message across.

I think Mr Davies must have noticed that I was pondering the situation, as he asked me just to carry on and said that what I was saying was quite right and that he was sure that his mother was communicating with him.

All this was fine and I went back to tuning in to the spirit lady. But then I was taken aback by what she said next: 'Tell him that Sheila is not going to die in February.'

Now I had no idea who Sheila was, but this wasn't the type of message the spirit world generally asked me to pass to people and I certainly wasn't willing to say it.

My sitter realized that I was holding back information and asked me to tell him what I knew. I tried to explain that I never give out information about dates of death and that the spirit people wouldn't really expect it of me. All the while I was trying to understand the situation and hoping that it wouldn't cause me to lose the link with the mother.

Eventually I just told Mr Davies that his mother said that Sheila would be fine. I know that was changing it a bit, but I really wasn't comfortable just blurting out the message as it was. Mr Davies, however, looked relieved and said, 'Thank God.' He told me that he had been hoping to hear this and that he had felt sure that if he contacted his mother she could lay his mind to rest.

There wasn't much more to the sitting and after a few bits of information about family members she had met on the other side, Mrs Davies just seemed to fade out. It was almost as though she had come in a burst of energy to get her message through and then gently faded back to her spiritual state.

I have been involved in many sittings, and indeed some really unbelievable situations, but this one turned out to be more important than I knew, for it liberated this man from the mental prison he had been in for the six months since his mother had died.

He told me that he had never had any belief in life after death, fortune-telling or anything psychic, but he had been out with some friends having a drink one day when a psychic had come into the pub and started to go round people and give out messages. Most people ignored her, but when she approached Mr Davies her opening statement was that his mother was going to die in the summer. To say that he was stunned would have been an understatement. Then she went on to say that his wife was going to die the following February, and this just blew his mind.

At this point the woman was taken by the arm by one of the bar staff and led out of the pub. Mr Davies's friends tried to rubbish the statements she had made, but he couldn't get them out of his mind. He felt violated in some way by the shocking statements she had made. He told me that he couldn't sleep that night and in the following months became an emotional wreck, especially when his mother became very ill in June 2006.

Sadly for Mr Davies, his beloved mother passed away less than a month afterwards. So now not only had he suffered this loss, but he had to endure the dark cloud of fear hanging over his head concerning his wife.

He had never told her about the predictions, but as he battled on alone, trying not to think about them, she became aware that there was something very wrong with him. At first she thought he was down because of the death of his mother, but his behaviour was such that her instinct told her that he was hiding something and eventually she forced him to talk to her about it.

Try to imagine for a moment what it would feel like to be told that two people you love and who are a huge part of your life are going to die within the space of a year. I honestly can't think what would possess someone, even if they had a psychic gift, to say such a thing. That fortune-teller had no compassion for the people she was giving messages to. People like this take no responsibility for their actions and it is my opinion that this type of 'psychic' does no more than make it up. On rare occasions the information does fit the person they are talking to, as had happened here, but I would say that that is no more than chance, not anything psychic, and certainly nothing to do with mediumship.

And the effect can be horrendous. By the time Mr Davies ended up sitting in front of me in December 2006 he had changed from being a level-headed, well-grounded and fun-loving happily married man with two beautiful children to a depressed and haggard shadow of himself who looked as though he had nothing much to live for. The pressure in his mind had become over-whelming and he felt helpless in the face of it.

When I had first looked at him, he had reminded me of so many people I see. He had seemed sad and confused and my first thoughts had been that he needed to be reconnected with a loved one. I had had no idea that he was carrying such a burden and that he had arrived at my door after much searching by his wife, who had seen me on a television programme talking about people like the psychic who had destroyed her husband's peace of mind. She had hoped that seeing a medium would help him to understand that what the woman had said to him was random and to stop worrying that she was going to die in the next two months.

It's no wonder that his mother in the spirit world came through in a blast of energy to tell him that that wasn't the case. I have no real idea how the spirit world knows some events in the future, but I do know that when it is necessary to bring healing or peace of mind to someone, they can see into our future lives and tell us enough to lay our fears to rest.

Subsequently, February 2006 came and went and Mrs Davies remained very much in this world, fulfilling her mother-in-law's prediction. Mr Davies changed back to the man he used to be and, on my advice, began living in the moment and enjoying each day as it came with his family. And for me, the message I passed on to him was another reminder of the responsibility that comes with being a medium and the way that messages can change people's lives.

CHAPTER 13

The message that changed my own life

THERE are many messages that stick out in my mind that have changed people's lives, some because they have brought closure to someone when there has been unfinished business between themselves and a loved one in the spirit world, and others because they have given a grieving person a sense of connection which has allowed them to go on with their own life, knowing that the spirit they contacted will always be watching over them, guiding them and waiting for them on the other side. It is difficult to choose one particular message that stands out, just one that has made a real difference to someone's life. Yet whenever I am asked to name a message that has changed my own life, the one that comes immediately to mind is one that made me lay my neck on the line for my belief – to go out on a limb, if you like.

It happened over ten years ago when Jim and I were living in Glasgow and working for the Spiritualist church there. There was a lady who came to us regularly for healing, and for the purpose of this book I'm going to call her Liz.

Liz had had cancer for some time and had undergone a lot of medical treatment. She had had several tumours removed from her body, as well as chemotherapy and reconstructive surgery. By the time we got to know her she had been through the wars. Each week she would come to the church to see Jim privately for spiritual healing, something he had practised for several years, as had I.

Within a short space of time, Liz started to feel better. She felt stronger in herself and noticed that her attitude was changing as well. All round, she was starting to feel more alive. The effect was confirmed by her consultant when she next visited the hospital. He told her that whatever she was doing she should keep it going, as her body was making a very good recovery. She even told us that he hadn't been shocked when she had mentioned that she had been having spiritual healing. Apparently he had gone on to explain to the student doctors in the room with them that energy never died and he couldn't rule out the possibility that someone might have the ability to reshape that energy while it was still in the body.

All in all, Liz was starting to feel a lot better about her life. I can't remember if it was on her next visit or the one after that, but it wasn't long before she was given the great news that her remaining cancer was in remission and that her consultant was happy to look at more reconstructive work. So happy was she at this news that she went out and took in a beautiful dog from an animal rescue centre. If her life had been saved, then she was going to try to save the life of another!

She continued to come to us for healing, and a friendship grew between us. She would bring her little dog too and she would spend her time play-fighting with our spaniel, Cheeky Charlie. All was well and Liz was looking to the future with a renewed sense of joy which she and her new companion shared, both having been given an extension to their lives.

Then everything changed. I remember to this day the feeling that ran through my body when Liz called me to tell me that she had been given very bad news. It was like being hit by a bolt of lightning. A routine X-ray on her jaw had showed a very advanced tumour connected to her optic nerve and which, sadly, was inoperable. She was told to get her affairs in order, as there was no hope for her.

It was one of the cruellest things I had ever heard. A lovely person had come through such turmoil, both physically and emotionally, and been given a reprieve only to have it snatched back and be forced to look death in the face all over again. This time, though, Liz had to consider her little dog. Her deepest concern was for her, not herself. She had prepared herself for dying so many times in the previous years that she had come to terms with it, but now she feared that her little dog would lose the chance to be loved and to be free and happy.

I went to see Liz two days later and offered to give her some healing. I don't really know what I expected to happen, but I remember thinking that I could ask the spirit world to bring her peace of mind. I suppose I just wanted to offer something to her at this time when hope wasn't really an option.

Now, it was the strangest thing. I had given spiritual healing to many people by that time and the sensation of warmth passing through my hands was always the first thing I experienced. Not on this occasion, though. As I stood behind my patient, hands on her shoulders, asking spirit to help her, I was very aware of someone standing beside me. He was someone I was very familiar with: my old friend Albert Best, one of the greatest mediums and healers of all time. Now he was in the spirit world, but his presence made me feel calm.

My eyes were closed and in my mind's eye I could see Albert pointing to Liz's head, just behind her left ear. I heard him say to me as clear as day: 'There's nothing there. They made a mistake.'

What did he mean?

I had no sooner sent out that thought to Albert than I heard him say, 'She will be told in ten days' time.'

To say I was gobsmacked would be an understatement. What should I do? One thing I don't believe in is giving people false hope. Liz had become a friend and, in any case, to give her a message like that would sound over-sympathetic and gushy, as if I was in denial and just couldn't accept what she had been told. So I really didn't want to give her the message from Albert. How could I?

As I stood there wondering what to do, Liz asked me if something had happened to me when I was healing her. She said that she had felt something strange but couldn't explain it.

I struggled not to mention what I had experienced, but I could still feel my old friend with me. And I trusted

Albert's mediumship more than that of any other medium I had ever met. I also trusted him as a man and a friend. In his own work he was astounding, but this was something which was very difficult indeed.

Then I just heard words coming out of my mouth: 'You're not going to die. They've made a mistake and in ten days' time you will be told that by your doctor.'

That was it, it was out and I couldn't take it back. It actually felt as though someone else had spoken, yet it had been my voice.

My eyes widened as I looked straight at Liz, wondering what she was going to say to this. The moment felt endless, nothing happened for what felt like an hour, yet probably only two or three seconds had actually passed when Liz burst out laughing. She just laughed and laughed.

'Thank you, Gordon,' she said. 'I know you mean well. Thank you for making me laugh, but nothing can be done for me now. Still, if nothing else, you gave me a laugh when everything was so serious.'

Her dog moved towards her and she held her close. I felt terrible. I wanted the ground to open up and swallow me. It was one of those moments in your life when you wish you could erase the last five minutes, but know that you have to live with what you have done. 'What a mistake,' I thought. All I wanted to do was put my arms round Liz and say sorry, but Albert hadn't finished yet. I began to speak to her again. Somehow I just couldn't shut up.

'In your bag you have a letter that no one but you knows about,' I said. 'This is from your brother, whom you haven't had any dealings with in years.' I knew that this message was coming directly from Albert now. 'If this is correct, then you must listen to what you have been told.'

Liz's face took on a new look now. She asked me how I knew that and who was giving this message. I took a moment to think about what was happening and then explained that Albert had been there during the healing and that I would never try to give her false hope but I felt sure that he was forcing this message through.

Then I heard myself say, 'You must trust this. Albert would never come to me with anything unless it was this important.'

I knew when those words passed through me that they were right. Then I felt Albert leave. Knowing the great man the way I did, I found myself trusting him more than what the doctors had told Liz.

In spite of that, I may tell you that I had many sleepless nights during the ten days that were to pass before Liz's next visit to the hospital. I also had many secret doubts that I never shared with anyone. Yet a part of me knew that what had happened that day was as much to get me to trust in my gift as it was for Liz to be given an unbelievable message.

On a Tuesday afternoon, ten days later, at 4 o'clock, my phone rang. It was Liz. 'You have gone way up in my estimations, mister!' were her words.

Believe it or not, the hospital had acknowledged that they had made a terrible mistake. They had been very apologetic at having put Liz through this horrendous episode and had explained that someone had looked at the wrong X-ray in the first place. There was no tumour and Liz was not going to die. Instead she and her little dog were going off to a remote place in the beautiful Scottish countryside for a much-needed break.

As for me, well, my belief in the spirit world had just increased beyond belief – and beyond the doubt which up to that point in my life had sometimes hung over me. My old friend Albert had come through and taught me a valuable lesson from the other side, a lesson that allowed me to take my gift to thousands of people in the years that followed. I didn't so much go out on a limb as was pushed there. But the trust I now have in what I do is what makes it special.

I do believe that that experience lifted me to another level of understanding of what I do. It wasn't long after that I started to travel further afield and work with many people all over the world. For me, it was a real life-changing event, a turning-point in how I trusted the spirit world. I saw how important the messages I passed on could be, and that encouraged me to work more with my gift.

*****

Through my work I have experienced so many life-changing experiences, none more so than the trip to South Africa where I was privileged to meet the wonderful children who inspired me to think of the importance of this life. Even when a life is short in this world it is important to live it. Everything is to live for, even death.

I believe that it is our experiences that make us who we are. Each hurt and pain shapes another little piece of our character and teaches us about life in this limited frame of human existence. I believe that we come down here to try as many limited experiences as we can in order to appreciate the freedom of our natural spiritual home on the other side.

In this life we may go through many changes, both good and bad, and experience both heaven and hell states. All of these let us know we are living. Each episode adds to our experience and once we have truly learned our lessons we will not have to endure them again.

This life is important to each of us and each of us is equally important to this life. And it's what we learn here that we take with us to the next life. The spirit messages reported here have been sent to show that life is continuous. That message of hope is for everyone who feels limited in this world, who feels sad or alone, disconnected or helpless. Life will eventually change. It's inevitable. This human world is one of impermanence. But remember, the one thing that will always exist is life itself, and what we call death is just a renewing of that life.

In any form of life, strive to be happy.

NOAH

Gordon Smith supports Noah (Nurturing Orphans of AIDS for Humanity), a South African charity formed in 2000 to help the 'epidemic of orphans' of the AIDS pandemic. The majority of these children are not HIV-positive and will need care into adulthood. Already they number one million but it is estimated that they will exceed two million by 2015 and will make up ten per cent or more of the country's population by 2020. The future of South Africa depends on what kind of citizens these orphans of AIDS grow up to be.

Noah works to support their growth into emotionally and psychologically stable adults. It helps them to develop into responsible and participative citizens, and enables them to become nurturing parents to their own children. It does this by mentoring enthused, driven and accountable individuals from the orphans' own communities to set up networks of care for these vulnerable children. Each network is known as an Ark.

Because Arks are run by volunteers equipped with the skills and confidence to provide care within their own communities, this empowers the communities and strengthens their capacity for care and support. This is more effective than care based on handouts, as well as being easier to administer and less prone to abuse. These factors mean that Noah's approach is highly cost-effective and sustainable, and can be rolled out throughout South Africa.

To find out more and to support Noah's work, visit www.noahorphans.org.za

Also Available by
Gordon Smith

Spirit Messenger

Read Gordon's first book, *Spirit Messenger*, and find out how he became a medium, what has influenced his spiritual development over the years and what it has been like to work with the scientific world. Full of numerous stories told in Gordon's down-to-earth style, *Spirit Messenger* is the beginning of the journey.

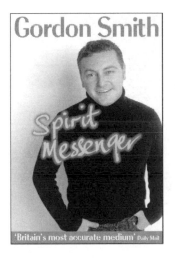

Don't forget you can find out more about Gordon Smith, his life, his work and his upcoming personal appearances by visiting his official website: www.psychicbarber.com.

The Unbelievable Truth

In this, Gordon's second book, he answers the questions he is most often asked by the people he meets. Gordon explains how the world of spirit works and how spirit communicates; he covers ghosts, hauntings, out-of-body experiences and much more. Ideal for anyone searching for more information on this huge subject area and a perfect accompaniment to *Through My Eyes* and *Spirit Messenger*.

Don't forget you can find out more about Gordon Smith, his life, his work and his upcoming personal appearances by visiting his official website: www.psychicbarber.com.

Through My Eyes

Thousands of people have come to Gordon seeking healing. From them he has gained a profound insight into the true nature of grief and our relationship with the spirit world. In this, his third book, join Gordon as he describes the true nature of grief, how it affects us and our loved ones who have crossed over. An uplifting and insightful book guaranteed to bring peace of mind to anyone that has been touched by loss.

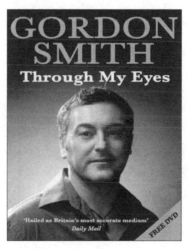

Don't forget you can find out more about Gordon Smith, his life, his work and his upcoming personal appearances by visiting his official website: www.psychicbarber.com.

Stories From The Other Side

This is Gordon's most personal and intimate book to date; in it he shares his experiences of growing up in Glasgow, his development as a medium and his extraordinary life working as a messenger for the spirit world.

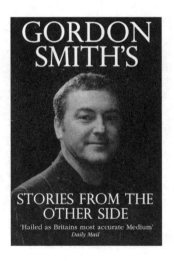

Don't forget you can find out more about Gordon Smith, his life, his work and his upcoming personal appearances by visiting his official website: www.psychicbarber.com.

5 Keys to Happiness Oracle Cards

Gordon and his close friend Tibetan Buddhist and artist Dronma have combined their skills and insights to create an oracle deck that they hope will help people to live happier lives. This extraordinary deck of cards fuses ancient Tibetan wisdom with contemporary Western psychological insight to give you the keys to achieving a happier and more balanced life. Using the five Tibetan elements of Earth, Water, Fire, Air and Space, this deck will help you understand the elemental forces, of which you and the world around you are composed. Use these 34 cards for daily guidance, individual spreads or meditation. Also included is a mandala image for guidance in laying out spreads.

Don't forget you can find out more about Gordon Smith, his life, his work and his upcoming personal appearances by visiting his official website: www.psychicbarber.com.

The Healing Power of Mediumship

In this fascinating double CD, Gordon explains the role of the medium in healing people's grief. The second CD includes meditations to increase your ability to tune in to the spirit world and send absent healing to anyone who is in need.

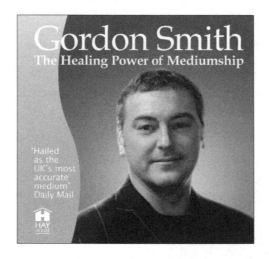

Don't forget you can find out more about Gordon Smith, his life, his work and his upcoming personal appearances by visiting his official website: www.psychicbarber.com.

An Introduction to the Spirit World – Live Workshop

On CD1 you can hear a live workshop in which Gordon describes his experiences of the spirit world and his development as a medium. He outlines the ways that the spirit world make their presence known to their loved ones, and explains ways of feeling closer to spirit.

In his down-to-earth and humorous style, Gordon explains some of the mechanics of mediumship and describes how psychics differ from mediums. Listening to this inspirational CD will enable you to gain a closer understanding of the work of a medium and help you to open up a deeper connection to the spirit world.

CD2 contains three guided meditations:

1. Listening to your inner voice and higher self
2. Connecting to your spirit guides
3. Sending compassion and healing to others.

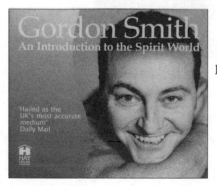

Don't forget you can find out more about Gordon Smith, his life, his work and his upcoming personal appearances by visiting his official website: www.psychicbarber.com.

Developing Mediumship – Live Workshop
2-CD Set

Let Gordon teach you how to start to develop your connection with the spirit world and begin to form a closer relationship with the spirits that are stepping forward to communicate with you.

Gordon will take you through meditations and exercises that will enable you to experience the difference between psychic ability and mediumship. In his warm and accessible style of teaching Gordon will encourage you to take the first steps in increasing your spiritual awareness and to begin to trust the truth of your own experiences.

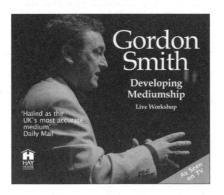

Don't forget you can find out more about Gordon Smith, his life, his work and his upcoming personal appearances by visiting his official website: www.psychicbarber.com.